Someone Out There Needs Me

ALSO BY ROBERT TUTTLE, JR. . . .

John Wesley: His Life and Theology

Someone Out There Needs Me

A Practical Guide to Relational Evangelism

Robert G. Tuttle, Jr.

ZONDERVAN PUBLISHING HOUSE
OF THE ZONDERVAN CORPORATION
GRAND RAPIDS, MICHIGAN 49506

Someone Out There Needs Me
Copyright © 1983 by The Zondervan Corporation
Grand Rapids; Michigan

Library of Congress Cataloging in Publication Data

Tuttle, Robert G., 1941–
Someone out there needs me.
Bibliography: p.
1. Evangelistic work. I. Title.
BV3790.T78 1983 253.7 83-10337
ISBN 0-310-36621-6

Unless otherwise indicated, the Scripture references are taken from *The Holy Bible; New International Version.* Copyright 1978 by New York International Bible Society. Used by permission.

Designed by Ann Cherryman
Edited by Edward Viening

Printed in the United States of America

83 84 85 86 87 88 / 10 9 8 7 6 5 4 3 2 1

to my sisters
Betty White and Kitty Boone

their witness to Jesus Christ
is proof enough of indispensability

Acknowledgements

Many people other than its author contribute significantly to the making of a book. Zondervan Publishing House deserves first notice. For several years this book simmered, cooking slowly, waiting for its time. The publishing team at Zondervan patiently monitored its journey from a good concept, through mediocre early drafts, to a book that I believe has great potential for assisting others in speaking a relevant word for Jesus Christ. To them I say thank you.

Although the early process was begun while I was teaching Evangelism and Wesleyan Studies at Fuller Seminary, the important final copy was done at Oral Roberts University. Provost and Vice-President for Academic Affairs Carl Hamilton, and Vice-Provost for Theological and Spiritual Affairs and Dean of the School of Theology Jim Buskirk encouraged me greatly, making available the word-processing center for both writing and editing. I am in their debt. I must also mention the particular efforts of Arlene Dewell whose hard work helped me to meet time lines week after week. Thank you as well to my secretary Joyce Featherston for much needed affirmation.

Finally, appreciation to Artie and the kids. Our sincere prayer is that it was all worthwhile.

Contents

Introduction 13

Part I. Establishing the Gospel Core

Chapter 1 Jesus Is Lord, What It Meant ... 19

Chapter 2 Jesus Is Lord, What It Means ... 27

Chapter 3 Developing Personal Guidelines 34

Chapter 4 A Case Study 42

Part II. Establishing a Sphere of Influence

Chapter 5 Messianic Complexes Die Hard 49

Chapter 6 I'm Indispensable 54

Chapter 7 Developing Personal Guidelines 58

Chapter 8 A Case Study 67

Part III. Meeting Felt Needs

Chapter 9 The Needy People 75

Chapter 10 Allowing Needs to Surface ... 80

Chapter 11 Applying God's Answer, Keep It Simple 86

Chapter 12 A Case Study 94

Part IV. Follow-up, the Indispensable Task
Chapter 13 Follow-up Through Continuing Relationships 103
Chapter 14 Follow-up Through Community 110
Chapter 15 Follow-up, the Role of the Spirit 118
Chapter 16 A Case Study 127

Conclusion 131
Bibliography 134

Someone Out There Needs Me

Introduction

The idea for this book was spawned in a moment. Recently, I had the privilege of sharing the platform at a national conference with several other persons, and three of us were to speak in rapid succession. The first to speak was a well-known evangelist. He captured us, and seemed to say all there was to say. I must admit I was a bit overwhelmed. As the next person rose to speak, she leaned over to me and whispered: "How do I follow *that*?" Then it hit me. I said to her what I had been feeling for some time but had never had an opportunity to state so pointedly: "Listen, you have a word to proclaim, and you have a sphere of influence where only you can minister most effectively. There are people here who the rest of us cannot reach nearly as easily as you can. Someone out there is waiting to hear it from *you*!" At the end of her presentation, she received a standing ovation.

Someone out there needs me. Someone out there needs *you*. And that is precisely what this book is all about. The gospel of Jesus Christ has to be communicated at many different levels on many different fronts. Most of the world is "gospel-proof" to any single approach. The evangelical slogan "One Way" refers to the person of Jesus Christ, not to our method of presentation. It is most important, therefore, to develop styles of evangelism that are solid, workable, and uniquely personal. Evangelism is more than technique; it is total lifestyle. As we learn to weave gospel bones into the flesh of our own experience, the world should not know where our living leaves off and our witness begins. Where evangelism is concerned, I keep asking myself and others certain questions. Each of the four parts of this book seeks to answer some of these questions. For example, evangelism has been defined as faithful proclamation of the gospel so as to evoke a response (yes or no); so why does the content of that "faithful proclamation" seem to vary from evangelist to evangelist? According to some, God seems to demand more. According to others, He seems to demand less. The problem lies in the apparent disparity between one and the other so, *what is the heart of the gospel*? To put is a bit negatively, what is the least I can believe and still be a Christian? Before answering we should realize that if the least is truly representative of God's claim on our lives, then the least is also the most. Can we require more than God would require?

Part I seeks to establish the basic content of the gospel. More than that, it also attempts to establish our own understanding of that content by suggesting certain guidelines that will keep us continually in touch with the heart of the Good News.

Part II then seeks to answer another set of questions. Once I understand the gospel, how do I present it to others? Early in my ministry I realized with certain clarity that, just because "I had the truth," there was no guarantee that the world would listen, at least to me. Too many people "out there" simply were not responding to my presentations of the gospel. Although my attempts to be "all things to all people" broadened the scope of my efforts, the number responding remained more or less constant. In spite of this however, I began to realize that some were responding to *my* presentations/proclamations/presence who were not responsive to others whom I had always thought to be more effective than myself. So, what are my particular gifts? Where do I minister most effectively? This part of the book therefore seeks to establish our own sphere of influence by suggesting certain guidelines that will keep us in touch with those who respond most easily to our particular ministry.

Part III seeks to bring these first two parts together. Effective evangelism is usually effective because it meets real need—and we all have needs. For example, I'm told that four out of five persons in this country alone do not like doing what they do. Their work is little more than making a living. The only thing they have to look forward to is a two-day weekend, a two-week vacation, or a sixty-inch base and twelve inches of powder snow on some ski slope. There has to be more to life than that. Evangelism can be propositional or relational. Proposition states the case. Here it is; take it or leave it. Most leave it. *Relational evangelism allows felt needs to surface out of a relationship and then the gospel speaks specifically to those needs.* Few things are more difficult than trying to convince some people of their need for the gospel. Why not get to know them personally? Why not allow trust to develop and then apply the Good News to an area where they sense the need for help?

Part IV concerns follow-up and discipleship. John Wesley once remarked: "How dare you lead people to Christ without providing an adequate opportunity for growth and nurture. Anything less is simply begetting children for the murderer." So, how do we sustain those who have been converted?

Having asked this, let me put all this into a larger perspective. As far as methods of evangelism are concerned, no attempt will be made in the book to be inclusive. The very nature of our primary thesis prevents us from stating "this is all there is to say, even about relational evangelism." Little mention is made, for example, of the more conventional approaches to evangelism except, perhaps, by way of contrast. The bibliography at the end of the book should suggest just how well those approaches have already been covered. The point is that many books on evangelism tend to neutralize our uniquenesses by giving the impression that their method alone is the "right" method of evangelization. Most of us know better. So, why not admit at the outset that each of us has to select a style that is consistent with who we are? Rather than state the definitive word, why not suggest certain guidelines adaptable to our many differences, the very differences that make us effective where only we can be most effective?

Also, there is little here designed to motivate us to evangelize as such. Admittedly, many of us need motivation but, again, books on that subject have already been written. It is just that at some point it is necessary to admit no one book can do it all, so one of my basic presuppositions is that many of us are already motivated to share our own understanding of the gospel and are simply looking for a fresh approach that can become uniquely me. I believe that an integral part of our own commitment is the desire to share with others what we have learned ourselves. Many of us have already been convicted by words like those from Ezekiel 3:

> Son of man, I have made you a watchman for the house of Israel; so hear the word I speak and give them warning from me. When I say to a wicked man, "You will surely die," and you do not warn him or speak out to dissuade him from his evil ways in order to save his life, that wicked man will die for his sins, and I will hold you accountable for his blood. But if you do warn the wicked man and he does not turn from his wickedness or from his evil ways, he will die for his sin; but you will have saved yourself.

Surely sharing implies something to share. Something to share implies sharing.

So, you might well ask, "Why is this book so important?" That is a fair question. Again, I believe that most of the body parts of the church are crippled, not only because they lack motivation, but because they also lack competence and know-how. Too many of us have little or no self-esteem. We fear rejection or feel an inability to talk about our faith clearly. So, this is another attempt to get the church thinking and moving evangelistically or (as Donald McGavran would say) to get her "off the pill." And, if all these things have been said before (if our principle is true), still someone out there needs to hear it from me. That, after all, is not simply an attempt at a clever book title. It is really what our several ministries and relational evangelism are all about.

Part I

Establishing the Gospel Core

Chapter 1
Jesus Is Lord, What It Meant

Evangelism is a cross in the heart of God.
Leighton Ford

If the gospel is not caught purely by osmosis, then evangelism at some point includes proclamation. But what is being proclaimed? What did Jesus and the early apostles preach and, equally important, what did their audiences hear? These and similar questions compel the serious student to establish solid principles for interpreting the biblical message.

THE TASK

Krister Stendahl's article in the *Interpreter's Bible Dictionary* entitled "Contemporary Biblical Theology" speaks of interpreting Scripture *empathetically*. His major thesis revolves around a dual theme—what it meant and what it means. We cannot know what the gospel message means until we first of all know what it meant. It is a poor hermeneutic to force the Scriptures to answer questions they were never asked. To state the same case a bit more positively, once we know what was actually being said, and what was actually being heard (what it meant), then we can apply the truth of that message faithfully to our contemporary scene (what it means). Empathy demands identification. Again, if human nature remains basically the same (as I suspect it does) we must first gain a clear understanding of what the core of the gospel is, and what it meant in the first century so that we can then know what it means for us today. So, our task is clearly before us. The remainder of this chapter will seek to establish that core and the next chapter will seek to apply its truth (however briefly) to the present.

THE CORE STATED

If I were asked to describe the content of the gospel as briefly as possible, I would simply say, "Jesus is Lord." Whatever it takes to communicate that thought could be considered the gospel core. Having said that, let us digress for a moment to state our rationale for establishing such a core, and then look to the Scriptures for support.

Each of us has at least some idea of what it means to be a Christian. We establish boundaries accordingly. Some of these boundaries are perhaps too narrow, some too wide. I once read the works of a Flemish mystic, Madame Antoinette Bourignon, who believed that there were fewer than twenty Christians in the entire world, and they all lived on her island. On the other hand, some of us interpret the gospel so loosely that we are like Robinson Crusoe's goat fence. He built it so wide that the goats on the inside of the fence were just as wild as those on the outside. Yet, when a person says, "I am a Christian," he or she confesses not only to the essentials of faith, but probably to some nonessentials as well. The point is that many of us in presenting the gospel do not realize that we present not only the core, but a great deal of baggage as well. This is not to imply that core is good and baggage is bad. Both are good. Baggage gains a hearing so that the core can convert. It is just that when we know what is essential (the core) and what relates only to our specific peculiarities (the baggage), we are far more likely to be consistent with the core and more flexible with the baggage. This consistency/flexibility gives us the freedom to be constant yet more sensitive to the particular needs of those to whom we seek to minister. Let me attempt a simpler description. Assume for a moment that the core of the gospel is in fact "Jesus is Lord," but that we also believe strongly that those who claim Jesus as Lord will then submit to baptism by immersion, affirm the infallibility of the Pope, and practice passivism. Since many of us will admit that we were converted before any such subsequent beliefs or doctrines even occurred to us the "Jesus is Lord" is the core and the remainder (though perhaps important) is baggage. Later on we will see that baggage has not only to do with content, but with who, where, and what we are as well. Here, however, the point is that some persons respond more easily to the kind of presentation that affirms not only the core but emphasizes baptism (Baptists), others the infallibility of the Pope (Catholics), and still others passivism (Mennonites). Relational evangelism focuses on the core but remains flexible with regard to the baggage. This is done in an attempt to be sensitive to those whom we seek to influence according to their particular situation. This is perhaps an oversimplification but it should serve as a point of departure (along with the accompanying diagram) to a concept not too easily understood. Now, let us turn to the core itself.

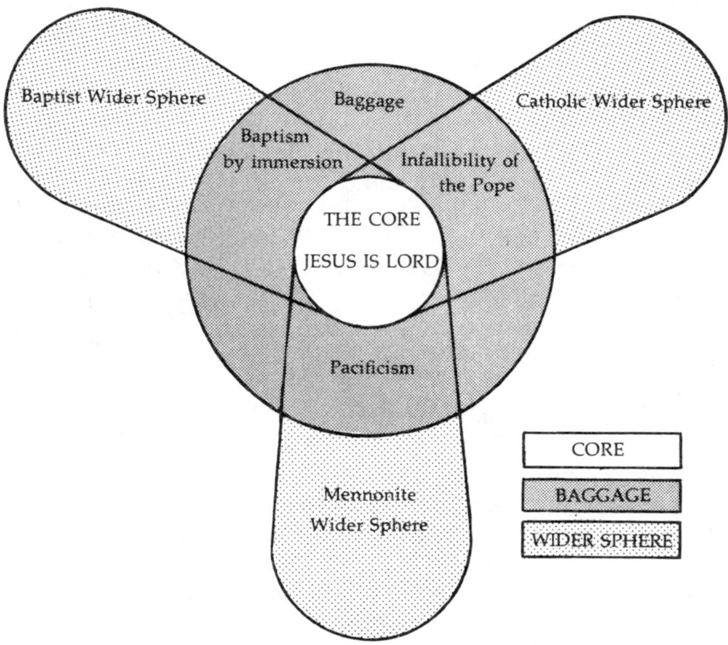

The Scriptures do suggest that there was indeed a corpus of belief taught by Jesus and the apostles that is essential for salvation. In fact, the heart of the Good News is more significantly Jesus Himself. Not that the stories about what He said and did are not important. They most certainly are. Jesus came preaching Good News to the poor. He proclaimed freedom for the prisoners and release to the oppressed. He healed the sick. In the final analysis, however, He proclaimed the year of the Lord's favor and, as the anointed One of God, He insisted that He was its fulfillment (Luke 4:17–21; cf. Isa. 61:1ff.). This was the news that shook the complacent, attracted the crowds, and turned the heads. It incurred the wrath of the people who threatened Him with stones and nailed Him to a cross. Jesus came proclaiming that the kingdom of God was at hand and that He was it. Origen insisted that Jesus was *the kingdom in person.* Let's look at the Scriptures themselves.

Matthew 21:42–44 is a good place to begin. The setting is the temple. The chief priests and elders have challenged the authority of Jesus. Jesus then tells them the parable of the two sons and the parable of the tenants in the vineyard. He concludes the latter by asking them, "Have you never read in the scriptures: 'The stone the builders rejected has become the capstone; the Lord has done this, and it is marvelous in our eyes'? Therefore I tell you that the kingdom of God will be taken away from you and given to a people who will produce its fruit. He who falls on this stone will be broken to pieces, but he on whom it falls will be crushed." Matthew then comments: "When the chief priests and the Pharisees heard Jesus' parables, they knew he was talking about them. They looked for a way to arrest him, but they were afraid of the crowd because the people held that he was a prophet" (21:45).

The One who came preaching was Himself the proclamation. Prophet, yes, but those who knew Him best knew that He was far more than that. John 4 and 9 tell interesting stories. Both the Samaritan woman and the man born blind acknowledge (enroute to a saving faith) that Jesus is at least a prophet (4:19; 9:17). That is never the end of the story, however. In both cases, Jesus admits to being the Messiah (4:26; 9:37) and in both cases the final response is to confess Him as Lord, the Savior of the world (4:42; 9:38).

All four Gospels exhort us to believe that Jesus is the Christ, the Son of the living God. In Matthew, for example, Jesus congratulates Peter on his confession of faith, "Blessed are you, Simon son of Jonah, for this was not revealed to you by man, but by my Father in heaven" (16:17).

Mark also exhorts his readers to receive Jesus as Lord. For example, in answer to the high priest's question, "Are you the Christ, the Son of the Blessed One?" Jesus replies: "I am, and you will see the Son of Man sitting at the right hand of the Mighty One and coming on the clouds of heaven" (14:61–62).

In Luke's Gospel even demons (4:41) and stones (19:40) threaten to bear witness to the lordship of Jesus. We also find a thief on a cross (23:42) looking to Jesus as the kingdom in person.

John's Gospel quotes Jesus saying: "I am the gate" (10:9); "I am the way and the truth and the life. No one comes to the Father except through me" (14:6). I do not know how He could make it any clearer. The heart of the gospel proclaims Jesus Christ as Lord. He was fully man. He was a prophet. At the same time He is fully God. He is the Christ, the Son of the most high God. The miracle of the Incarnation begins with an empty womb and concludes with an empty tomb.

I was in London recently. Near my hotel I met a young Muslim (some say that there are more Muslims in London now than Christians). After getting acquainted, I asked him about the Islamic law. Although I knew something about it already, I was still amazed. I thought the Judeo-Christian law was tough. The Islamic law is far tougher. You break that law and they take your hand off, or your head. After some time I asked my Muslim friend if he would like to be able to fulfill such a law. He said yes. My reply? I asked him to listen to a story. The story I told him was (you guessed it) the story of Jesus. I believe He is the answer to every law. I have never tried to defend Christianity as just another code, for Christianity picks up where every other religion leaves off. It doesn't speak just of the law, but of grace to fulfill the law. My Muslim friend, like the Samaritan woman and the man born blind, began to move beyond Jesus as prophet (as most Muslims readily acknowledge) to Jesus as Lord.

Now that we have glanced at the Gospels, let us touch base for a moment with some of the earliest apostolic preaching. The sermons preached by Peter in the Book of Acts are a productive source. Five sermons in Acts have been attributed to Peter (2:14–39; 3:12–26; 4:8–12; 5:29–32; 10:34–47). All five (the first four were directed specifically to Jewish audiences) involve four basic proclamations. First, the authoritative proofs of the Christ event are cited (the Old Testament prophecy is fulfilled; God's activity in the Christ event is described; the apostolic eyewitness is mentioned; and the miracles are proclaimed). Second, the Christ event

ANALYSIS OF PETER'S SERMONS

Proclamations:	Acts 2:14–39	Acts 3:12–26	Acts 4:8–12	Acts 5:29–32	Acts 10:34–47
Authoritative proofs of the Christ event					
1. OT prophecy fulfilled	16–21, 25–28, 30, 34–35	22–24	11		43
2. God's activity described	22, 24	15	10		38
3. Apostolic eyewitnesses	32	15		30	30, 42
4. Miracles proclaimed	4, 22, 23	16	10	32	
Proclamation of the Christ event					
1. Jesus' humanity	22	13, 23, 26			
2. Jesus' ministry	22	16, 21, 18			38
3. Jesus' crucifixion	23	12–15, 18	10	30	39
4. Jesus' resurrection	24	15	10	30	40
5. Jesus' exaltation	33	16, 21		31	
6. Jesus is Lord	36	16, 20, 22, 23	11, 12	31	40
Our involvement					
1. Particularly Jewish	22, 30, 33	25, 26	10, 11	30	
2. All should know about it	23, 26	23	10	31	41–43
3. Response determines destiny—repent and be baptized	38	19	12	31	43
Benefits of a right response					
1. Forgiveness	38	19	12	31	43
2. Refreshing		19			
3. The Holy Spirit	38			32	44
4. Christ's Return		20			

itself is described (His humanity, ministry, crucifixion, resurrection, exaltation, and lordship). Third, Peter insists on our own involvement in the Christ event (since it was particularly Jewish, the Jews should know about it, but what is more important, our response determined our destiny—repent and be baptized). Finally, the benefits of a right response are enumerated (forgiveness, a refreshing, a gift of the Holy Spirit, and Christ's return). The chart on page 24 demonstrates the particular verses as they relate to these proclamations.

From these proclamations we can see clearly that the core of the apostolic message is that sequence of redemptive events that sweeps the hearers along with compelling logic toward the climactic confession that *Jesus Christ is Lord* (Acts 2:36).

To put all of this in still another way, C. H. Dodd summarizes the early apostolic teaching in six major statements:

1. The age of fulfillment has dawned.
2. This has taken place through the ministry, death, and resurrection of Jesus.
3. By virtue of the Resurrection, Jesus has been exalted at the right hand of the Father.
4. The Holy Spirit in the church is the sign of Christ's presence, power, and glory.
5. The messianic age will shortly reach its consummation in the return of Christ.
6. An appeal for repentance, the offer of forgiveness, and the promise of salvation.[1]

To summarize, we began this chapter by stating our task. As evangelists we must have a clear understanding of the essence of the gospel (the core). Failure to do so frequently leads to additions beyond the demands of Scripture (our baggage). If, however, we are consistent with our understanding of the core, then we are free to be flexible with our baggage, thus increasing our sphere of influence. Again, although the essential gospel once understood must be communicated consistently, our specific peculiarities enable us to minister more and more effectively within an ever-widening circle of friends who desperately need to know that Jesus is Lord.

In all of the passages mentioned, perhaps the gospel message can best be summarized by Peter's words in his first sermon: "Therefore let all Israel be assured of this: God has made this Jesus, whom you crucified, both Lord and Christ" (Acts 2:36). In short, the proclamation—Jesus is Lord! The appeal—therefore change your attitude toward God!

---

[1]C. H. Dodd, *The Apostolic Preaching & Its Developments* (London: Hodder & Stoughton, 1963), pp. 21ff.

Chapter 2
Jesus Is Lord, What It Means

Evangelism is God's extension of His grace through believers who engage in sharing the life of Christ with others. Myron S. Augsburger

I had a student from Uganda, and one Christmas she went to a shopping center here in Tulsa and began to ask shoppers (as though she were uninformed): "What is Christmas all about?" The replies: Santa Claus! Then she returned to Uganda and began asking some of her Muslim friends the same question. The replies: Christ's birthday. While not disparaging of Old Saint Nick, the point is that there is sometimes a considerable gap between what it meant and what it means.

When the people of the first century proclaimed Jesus as Lord, they believed Him to be the appointed Messiah, the Holy One of God. Unfortunately, many of those hearing such a word misunderstood the nature and mission of their Messiah. The Jews especially expected an all-conquering hero (a political Santa Claus) who could overthrow Roman oppression. The victory that God intended, however, was far greater than a mere military coup. The sacrifices were also far greater.

A NEW COVENANT

The coming of the Messiah was indeed the fulfillment of a new age. Under the old covenant (Old Testament) a sacrifice was required to emphasize the deadliness of sin. Sin, the great deceiver, always promises what it can never produce. It separates, and since God cannot bear to see His creations separated, He demanded a sacrifice to remind Israel that sin destroys life. So, the faithful confirmed and reconfirmed their covenant with God by preparing "burnt offerings and sin offerings." The result, however, was less then complete. Picture this:

James and John make their way to the temple in order to offer their sacrifices. James is a wealthy merchant, John a blind beggar. James brings with him a prime heifer, John a tiny bird. As they approach the altar, James catches sight of John out of the corner of his eye, and without thinking, swells with pride, feeling (quite unintentionally) himself better than John. The point is that the very thing that God instituted to draw the nation together through repentance and faith was often serving to divide. Hebrews 10:1 describes the problem: "The law is only a shadow of the good things that are coming—not the realities themselves. For this reason it can never, by the same sacrifices repeated endlessly year after year, make perfect those who draw near to worship." The old covenant always anticipated the new. Law must anticipate grace.

Jeremiah 31:31, therefore, had prophesied a new covenant. In the new covenant (New Testament) God Himself provides a sacrifice; He allows His only son to be nailed to a cross and creates level ground beneath it. The veil in the temple was ripped from top to bottom enabling all of us to receive the forgiveness of God by the same means. Furthermore, the sacrifice of Jesus not only established common means, it ensured our victory over sin and death *once for all.* Hebrews 10:19–22 says it well: "Therefore, brothers, since we have confidence to enter the Most Holy Place by the blood of Jesus, by a new and living way opened for us through the curtain, that is, his body, and since we have a great priest over the house of God, let us draw near to God with a sincere heart in full assurance of faith, having our hearts sprinkled to cleanse us from a guilty conscience and having our bodies washed with pure water."

Again, the victory created by the new covenant was far greater than a military coup. It overthrew the forces of evil and won the hearts of those who would put their faith and trust in Jesus Christ.

GOOD NEWS/BAD NEWS/GOOD NEWS

To state this a bit differently, the gospel of Jesus Christ involves good news, bad news, good news. The first good news is that we were created in the image of God. The first man and woman had fellowship with God, and *original righteousness.* They were without shame, unafraid. The bad news is that we have lost that God-created image. We have a propensity to evil, an *original* sin, and since sin cannot bear the light, we hide from God. The old covenant established a temporary covering for such sin but this covenant had to be renewed with continual sacrifice year after year. God then initiated a new covenant. That is the second good news. "God so loved the world" should never become a mere cliché. It is rooted in reality. God Himself has paid the price for a new and permanent covenant that is sufficient not only to provide a temporary covering for sin (propitiate), but also a permanent solution to root out sin (expiate). "Therefore, if anyone is in Christ, he is a new creation; the old has gone, the new has come! All this is from God, who reconciled us to himself through Christ and gave us the ministry of reconciliation" (2 Cor. 5:17–18).

Having said this let me hasten to add that all three parts of this gospel presentation are essential. Some omit the first good news. Their gospel is simply bad news/good news. Salvation, however, is far more than the forgiveness of sins; it is restoring us to our original rightousness—"without holiness no one will see the Lord." Others omit the bad news. Their gospel is simply good news/good news. They refuse to believe that our sin is serious enough to warrant separation from God or man. Still others omit both the bad news and the second good news. In this instance good news without bad news is no news. They believe that there is no need for reconciliation since God is "all loving" and would not allow our sins to cause separation in the first place.

How does all of this relate to the contemporary scene? We suggested earlier that human nature remains more or less constant. We in the twentieth century are just as much a part of the God-created image as were those in the first century. We too have a propensity to sin that leads inevitably to separation from God, from ourselves, and from those around us. In a phrase, we too are candidates for salvation. Leslie Brandt, in his book, *Great God, Here I Am,* writes:

> If I am up against something that is too much for me; if there are problems, weaknesses, sins, distortions in my life that I cannot solve or overcome; if I am lost in the wilderness of my own failure and insufficiencies—then I am eligible for the tour.[2]

THE WORLD WE LIVE IN

I have sometimes said, "Be slow to trust seminary professors who have been teaching more than five years. They tend to forget what the rest of the world is about." Since I am one of those professors I try to be especially sensitive to what is happening "out there." I try to read most of the best sellers. I ask questions, lots of questions. Frequently, I find myself talking to strangers. I want to know who they are, what they are thinking, and what is important to them. Would you like to know what I have found out? They are being "ripped off." The world has sold them a bill of goods, especially the mass media and the books that they read.

Some months ago on a cross-country flight I sat next to a woman who was reading a current best seller that I had read some weeks earlier. Its main thrust had to do with getting to the top. So what if we have to step on a few heads along the way? Who will know the difference 6,000 years from now? As I was grading papers (the old professor's usual posture), she was reading her book with apparent relish. After a couple of hours I asked her what she thought of the book. Quite frankly her response startled me: "Oh, I think it is great!" I then asked her about her occupation. She answered: "I am a buyer for a large department store back east." My next questions were my last: Did she have persons working under her? (Yes, 30), and How many of them subscribed to the philosophy of her new book? For the next two hours she talked nonstop, and by the time we landed in Los Angeles she had surrendered her new philosophy and was ready to burn the book. You see, those who worked under her, who subscribed to the "me first" philosophy, were not trustworthy. She could not turn her back on them without considerable anxiety. So help me, without so much as a word from me she convinced herself that the author of that book was dead wrong. That experience set me thinking—here are some of my conclusions.

Like that woman, much of the world on the surface is hedonistic, feeling-oriented, and sensualistic. Everywhere the pleasure principle is propagated. "If it feels good, do it!" is more than a psychological catch phrase. It has become an American way of life. Our senses are stimulated at every turn. Touch that, taste this, smell, hear, see the delightful things that we have created for your pleasure and all for no money down and low monthly installments. Low monthly installments indeed! I watched a member of a church I once served "install" himself into bankruptcy. It has become a national obsession and a recession is threatening to prove it.

Yet, below all of this the world out there has other problems. I believe that we are not only hedonistic, feeling oriented, and sensualistic, but lonely, fearful, insecure, and lost. Notice, the problems we face are not so much intellectual (if we will believe some of the "come ons" that are with us, we will believe anything). Rather, the problems we face focus on the human spirit and emotions. WAIT! This next point is so important, let's start a new paragraph to set it off.

If we understand properly what it meant that Jesus is Lord, then, *as Christians we proclaim a gospel that meets peoples real needs better than anyone else.* For example, most of us do not really want a lot of money. If the choice is wealth or the love of a caring companion, we will choose love, hands down. "What it meant" relates to a needy people, but the need is far deeper than some of us imagine. God in Jesus Christ is the friend who sticks closer than a brother. He is not nearly so much in the business of making us prosperous as He is in bringing people into meaningful relationships with one another. Thus, when my traveling companion got in touch with the truth, she was well on her way to finding her own solution.

THE COMPETITION

Just because we believe that Christianity has the only real answer to the world's needs does not mean that we go unchallenged. The competition/opposition is formidable. In fact, we make it so. Again, one of the reasons why we must get in touch with what it meant is to get in touch with what it means. When we do our research properly, we see the deeper, more sensitive issues of the spirit and emotions. On the other hand, when we fall into the trap of "trying to outworld the worldly" we make ourselves vulnerable. If, however, we go to the root of the problems, we are really without challenge. Believe it! Proclaim it! Accept it!

The gospel of the first century received a remarkable response because it led from strength. Its strength was its ability to meet ultimate need—our alienation from God. Today, we must continue to lead from strength. The competition meets surface needs; we meet ultimate needs. The competition plays to the senses; we speak to the mind and spirit. This is not to say that God cannot meet our more mundane needs as well. He can, most assuredly! It is just that the final word remains "seek first his kingdom and his righteousness, and all these things will be given to you as well." Let me illustrate.

Look at the so-called Third World. Let us take Africa, for example. There are presently 80 million animists in Africa alone. Sociologists tell us that during the next twenty years animism will no longer be a viable alternative for most African believers. Animism ascribes conscious life to all natural objects. Animists believe that mountains, plants, and even stones are inhabited by souls that may exist in a separate state. The result of all this is that as animists are exposed to education and other forms of thought that would tend to expel their ideas, they tend to look elsewhere for explanations that satisfy more adequately. So, by the year 2,000 nearly 80 million people will be looking for new answers to important questions.

Furthermore, these same people will be changing in other ways as well. Many will be relocated. Their political structures will change rapidly. Changing people are open to new ideas. History proves that people in flux began to ask the larger questions about the important issues of life in general. They reevaluate what is happening to them. Those with possible answers will at least get a hearing. You can well believe, however, that Christians will not be the only ones looking for an audience. Nearly 80 million animists will have to choose among such options as secularism, materialism, communism, Islam, and Christianity.

So, what do we offer them in the name of Jesus? The larger context for the words quoted above: "Seek first his kingdom and his righteousness," provides the answer. Do we offer them prosperity? Jesus says, "No one can serve two masters. . . . You cannot serve both God and Money." Do we offer them the "good life"? Jesus answers: "Therefore I tell you, do not worry about your life, what will you eat or drink; or about your body, what you will wear. Is not life more important than food, and the body more important than clothes?" Do we offer them power to work miracles? Jesus says: "Many will say to me on that day, 'Lord, Lord, did we not prophesy in your name and in your name drive out demons and perform many miracles?' Then I will tell them plainly, 'I never knew you. Away from me, you evildoers!'" Do we offer them pious platitudes? Again, the words of Jesus: "Not everyone who says to me, "Lord, Lord,' will enter the kingdom of heaven, but only he who does the will of my father who is in heaven." To put all of this another way in light of what it means, do we extol an American way of life? No! That plays into the hands of materialism. Do we discuss the virtues of free enterprise? No! That plays into the hands of secularism. Do we speak of democracy? No! That plays into the hands of communism. Do we argue the protestant ethic? No! That plays into the hands of Islam. All of those things (though perhaps noble in a way) argue the point in the wrong arena. Little wonder Paul exhorts in Ephesians 6:11–12: "Put on the full armor of God so that you can take your stand against the devil's schemes. For our struggle is not against flesh and blood, but against the rulers, against the authorities, against the powers of this dark world and against the spiritual forces of evil in the heavenly realms." In short, we need not fight this battle with conventional weapons. We offer the world a vital relationship with a living God who insists that *Jesus Christ is Lord!*

In conclusion, still another factor will play a prominent role here. Once committed, people's attitudes are extremely difficult to change. The time is *now,* not only for the Third World, but for the western world as well. I recently heard Alan Walker of Australia say that the toughest mission field is in the West. Here, the competition has already made its mark known. As Christians, we must engage the help of the Spirit. He alone gives us the needed advantage, an advantage that God intended us to use wisely. So, why play into the hands of the enemy? We must get back in touch with the heart of the gospel (the core) and stay in touch if we are to do battle effectively. The next chapter will suggest ways of developing personal guidelines for getting in touch, and staying in touch, with the essential gospel.

---

[2]Leslie Brandt, *Great God, Here I am* (St. Louis: Concordia Publishing House, 1969), p. 27.

Chapter 3
Developing Personal Guidelines

Evangelism is so making Christ known to men, that each is confronted with the necessity of personal decision, yes or no?
World Council of Churches–Amsterdam

This chapter concludes our exploration of the core of the gospel—"the least one can believe and still be a Christian." The remaining chapter of Part I is a case study designed to demonstrate the importance of establishing such a core.

In chapter 1 we sought to establish what it meant that "Jesus is Lord." There we saw that this truth was the final word throughout the New Testament. So, whatever it takes to communicate that could be considered the core of the gospel. Then, in chapter 2, we sought to demonstrate, however, briefly, just how relevant that core is for the contemporary scene. The gospel of Jesus Christ meets the needs of people at a level where it is without equal. Although on the surface the competition is fierce, below the surface, where lives can be changed radically, the Christian alone has the answer. Presumptuous? Perhaps, but that is what I believe. That is what motivates me. At some point we must be willing to disagree with those who will not affirm the absolute uniqueness of our faith in Christ. Listen, I know full well that truth is truth regardless of what I think truth is. Truth has never changed to accommodate what I believe truth to be. Truth remains truth. For that matter God remains God. If, for example, God is a triangle and I think He is a circle, He will not become a circle to accommodate what I believe Him to be. He remains a triangle. Nonetheless, at some point I must look people full in the face and say: "We may both be wrong, but we cannot both be right. We disagree." If I were ever forced to yield my faith in Jesus Christ, I believe that I would cease to exist. Flesh would no longer cling to bone. I could be poured into a basket. That is just how much of me is at stake. I have put my hand to the plow and there is no turning back.

The world is weary of trivial answers to important questions. Our entire western world, for example, has locked itself into a five-dimensional box—height, width, depth, time, and motion. Anything beyond those dimensions is held as suspect. If it cannot be seen, smelled, touched, tasted, or heard, we have been led to believe that it does not exist. The same principle applies to the left and right sides of the brain. Again, we are left-brain oriented. We are affirmed with regard to those functions (cognitive and rational) that relate to only our left hemisphere. The right hemisphere (creative, intuitive, and spiritual) is rarely stimulated, however, For example, when my young son was found to be gifted with numbers, he skipped the first grade. When he told his friends that he believed in angels, they laughed at him. The point is that important questions (a right-brain function beyond our five-dimensional box) deserves serious answers. Again, the gospel of Jesus Christ is not simply a philosophy of life. It is a way of life involving a personal relationship with a living God. It breaks us out of our confinement and throws us, we hope screaming with delight, into even greater realities that can be comprehended only by a larger world view. Having said this by way of review, we are ready for the task at hand.

THE RATIONALE FOR ESTABLISHING GUIDELINES

Guidelines are all around us. The various media talk about them constantly. Recently I saw guidelines established by the Supreme Court for racial integration in the cities and states. Congress outlined new guidelines for educational programs. The President spoke about guidelines for foreign policy. Like it or not, we all need boundaries.

Guidelines among Christians can either divide or unite. Without them we could never ordain our pastors. Church-school teachers would lack the needed focus to invest their time wisely. Evangelism would so burden the hearer with the nonessentials of left-brain trivia that little would be accomplished. It would constantly raise more questions than it would ask. It would lack the kind of thrust needed to negotiate the various "winds of doctrine" that can suddenly drop a person out of his or her intended course.

The primary thesis of this book has been that no one method alone is sufficient for the task of evangelism. Although the core, properly understood, is more or less constant, the means of communicating that core vary from person to person. This chapter seeks to establish guidelines that will enable the reader to get in touch with the core (or at least with his or her own understanding of it) and then remain in touch throughout his or her ministry (lay or otherwise) as a follower of Jesus Christ.

You might ask: "Once I have established the core, why must I then develop guidelines for staying in touch?" The answer is simple. We have faulty memories. We forget so easily. Our spheres of influence change. As our spheres of influence change, we sometimes tend to alter the core as well. Every three or four years I find myself needing to get back to the basics in order to sharpen my evangelistic message. I have found that certain guidelines serve to reestablish the essentials.

A WORD OF CAUTION

We all use guidelines whether we are aware of it or not. If we are aware of it, we can then test them in order to make certain they are solid and workable. Again, to distill the absolute essence of the Christian faith is to have already developed guidelines. In practice, this is how all of us evaluate doctrine. We have either explicitly or implicitly conceived an idea of what the bare essentials of Christianity are, and we have measured this idea against these guidelines.

So, since we all use guidelines, why not be aware of them? Why not make certain that our guidelines are complete enough to prevent our "baggage," our additions, our interpretation, from contradicting or fundamentally altering the meaning of the gospel.

A well-known theologian once commented that "Christ's death washed away our sins and disabled death." He went on to say that this we must believe, but that we could take or leave any explanation of how His death accomplished this according to our own understanding. Such a statement is freighted with a certain intuitive plausibility, but with a danger as well. The problem is that any "essential" statement derives the bulk of its meaning and substance from the "interpretations" that we apply to it. The interpretation might be an accurate one (consistent with what it meant) but it might also be an inaccurate one.

Much of the controversy in the church has not been over the core so much as to how that core is interpreted or misunderstood. The reason for the controversy has not been that one side necessarily wanted to manipulate the other, but that each side clearly felt that the other's interpretive "baggage" fundamentally altered the basic meaning of the gospel. When I was a student in seminary the "God is dead" debates were raging. Many who argued such a viewpoint were arrogant and self-seeking, but a few were both humble and sincere. Van Buren's *Secular Gospel,* for exmaple, took seemingly basic gospel content and developed an understanding that made no reference whatever to God or to the supernatural. In fact, Van Buren, who may have been misguided, but was certainly no idiot, proposed to be more Christian in his interpretation than either some neo-orthodox theologians or left-winged theists.

The question is: Do our guidelines simply state the case or do they state it in such a way as to include a metaphysical system (a supernatural one) consistent with what it meant? Any set of guidelines must ensure the kind of interpretation that is consistent with the mind-set of Jesus but without succumbing to the rigid scholasticism that attempts to make *everything* essential. Fundamentalists rightly see the danger in allowing too much room for interpretation; so they tend to nail everything down as tightly as possible. Consequently, many fundamentalists are not concerned with essentials and nonessentials. Everything is essential. They want the right answers and they feel that they have come fairly close by properly studying the Scriptures. If one were to question them about how "essential" one particular doctrine is, they would respond immediately that it is essential to be as true to God's Word as possible. They happily discuss how scriptural a particular doctrine is, but not how essential. I confess I am somewhat sympathetic with their approach, but it lays a terrific burden on the evangelistic task. The doctrines that come out of this are so bound together that to deny (or even omit) any part of the "fundamental" theology (no matter how small) is to reject the whole.

The point is that it is difficult to separate the core from the baggage. Again, however, it is a necessary effort. Relational evangelism insists that we be constant with the core, but flexible with the baggage. So let us restate the core briefly and then suggest some possible guidelines employed in making such a statement.

THE CORE RESTATED

In chapter 1 we established that at the heart of the matter is the fundamental assertion that "Jesus is Lord." This means that we have a Messiah who when properly understood and received delivers us from sin and restores us to our original righteousness, so fulfilling the nature of the new covenant. This gospel necessarily involved the following doctrines:

> The *nature of God:* there is one God who is personal and who is the Creator of all things. In communicating this, we should stress the aspects of a God who cares *for* and is involved *with* His creation.
>
> The *nature of man:* at some point we must acknowledge the seriousness of our problem. We are out of harmony with our personal Creator. We are separated and can be reconciled only by God Himself.
>
> The *uniqueness of the person and reconciling work of Jesus Christ:* both the person and work of Jesus Christ are unique. Only through Him can we be reunited with God. In order to grasp the significance of this, we must have at least some understanding of His humanity and His deity—God in Jesus Christ reconciling the world to Himself.

THE GUIDELINES

The actual guidelines to follow are only *suggested* principles that have served me across the years. At this point I want to emphasize the need for each of us to develop these for ourselves.

After saying all of this it seems almost anticlimactic to admit that the guidelines used for measuring the above can be grouped under three simple headings: Is it biblical? Is it necessary? Does it work?

Is it biblical? Essential doctrine should be taken directly from the Scriptures rather than from a specific theological system or from the confessions of a particular denomination.

Two examples should be adequate to introduce this point.

In Book III of John Calvin's *Institutes* he states that God has predestined some to heaven and some to hell. His followers later made this doctrine, called double predestination, an essential part of Calvinism. While some biblical evidence may exist for such a doctrine, many have come to salvation in Jesus Christ without such knowledge. Remember, the issue here is not to argue whether or not the doctrine is truth but to state simply that such doctrines are not essential for salvation.

The second example is the doctrine of biblical inerrancy. Although I myself hold to a form of biblical inerrancy, few other doctrines have caused such confusion and dissension, especially among evangelicals. Many of those seeking to defend such a position argue that God always does what is right. This is correct. Therefore, God must have done it this way. Obviously the middle statement, "what is right," involves another whole set of criteria hidden to the original argument. Essential doctrine must first come from Scripture, not from some particular system or thought process.

On a more positive note, we might well add that essential doctrines manifest certain other characteristics as well. For example, these doctrines receive repeated emphasis in Scripture. In chapter 1 we noted that "Jesus is Lord" was repeated in one form or another in every sermon Peter preached. The New Testament writers had no exclamation point to direct their readers' attention to an important subject. Instead, they simlpy repeated those doctrines and events that were particularly significant. Luke, for example, in the Book of Acts, refers to Paul's conversion three times.

Another principle related to this is that essential doctrine would have been stressed by Jesus in His earthly ministry. His repeated emphasis on God as father, and His own death and resurrection, give us immediate clues.

Finally, from a biblical perspective, essential doctrine (again as seen in chapter 1) should have an apostolic precedent. Was it preached early enough to have come from the Lord Himself?

Is it necessary? The omission of an essential doctrine would distort the gospel. Some doctrines of the Christian faith are so fundamental to our presentation that when viewed together, they tend to place it "in focus." For example, no gospel presentation would be complete without mention of the resurrection of Christ. Some so-called Christians acknowledge His death, but fail to realize fully the significance of His resurrection. The Scriptures hold this doctrine so precious that entire books (John) and sections of books (1 Cor. 15) are devoted to bringing us to faith in the bodily resurrection. Admittedly, the "body" that came out of the tomb was different than the body that went into the tomb. The body that came out could appear and disappear at will. Our contention is, however, that although the body was different, the Lord left nothing behind. We should realize that the stone was rolled away not to let Jesus out but to let us in that we might see with our own eyes what God had done—that we might believe.

The other side of this issue insists that many doctrines are perhaps important, but are not essential to salvation itself. The thief on the cross was received without baptism. The Samaritans in Acts 8 were converted without knowledge of the indwelling power of the Holy Spirit. Most of us were led to Christ without a great deal of the theology that we adhere to today. Little wonder Karl Barth writes that "theology [to use Anselm's expression] is faith seeking understanding."

Does it work? A final guideline simply asks if the given presentation affects the kind of change that can be attributed only to the power of God. Such a pragmatic approach seems a bit mundane, yet the issue is just that simple. Those who responded to Peter's sermons, for example, were obviously converted. Their lives demonstrated change. The fruit of the Spirit was manifested in their communities. The gifts of the Spirit were revealed throughout their ministries. They clearly demonstrated that the same power available to Jesus was available to them as well. In short, the gospel produced. This is not to say that the presentation itself must elicit change. Evangelism can still be evangelism and be rejected as such. When received, however, the gospel we preach must produce what it promises—a new life empowered by the Holy Spirit.

Let us summarize this chapter. We all need boundaries. Where evangelism is concerned a lack of focus burdens the message with the nonessentials of left-brain trivia. A word of caution was then brought to ensure that our Gospel core does not simply state the case, but that it states it in such a way as to include a metaphysical system (a supernatural one) consistent with the mind-set of Jesus. We then restated the core in terms of the nature of God, the nature of man, and the uniqueness of the person and reconciling work of Jesus Christ. Then, the guidelines were grouped under three simple headings: Is it biblical? Is it necessary? Does it work? Here again we are reconfirmed in our conviction that at the heart of the biblical message, taught by the gospel writers, preached by the apostles, and proclaimed by the church, is the fundamental assertion that *Jesus is Lord*!

Chapter 4
A Case Study

At the end of each of the four parts of this book a case study will be presented in order to illustrate the major points of the three previous chapters. Since Part I discusses the "core of the gospel" the following study has been designed as a teaching aid (to be taught in the classroom or to be used as illustrative material) demonstrating the importance of establishing such a core.

THE CASE: "ALL IN GOOD TIME"

Tom Hamilton, a young pastor, sat listening intently to Amy the young girl sobbing in front of him. It was 12:45 Sunday morning. They sat in a small waiting room outside the intensive care unti in a local hospital. Visitors were allowed into the ICU on the hour, one at a time, but only for ten minutes. Earlier that night Amy and her boy friend Peter Mullins had been involved in an automible accident. She had been treated for minor cuts and bruises and released, but Pete had been severely injured and the prognosis was not good. His internal injuries were so serious that most of his major organs were not functioning properly. Although he had an occasional moment of consciousness the chances that he would survive the night were slim.

Pete's parents had just stepped out of the waiting room leaving Amy and Tom alone. She immediately drew him aside and while sobbing said, "There is something I must tell you. I know Pete's parents think he is a good Christian but I am not so sure. Just recently he has started to agree with his parents and no longer believes that he must have faith in Jesus. All that is necessary, he claims, is to believe in God. Christ was a man, a prophet maybe, but nothing more. Tom, I'm worried. Is it enough simply to believe that God is? Although he does not know it, Pete is dying. Can you say something to him—please!"

Background

Tom Hamilton is the pastor of New Hope Congregational Church. He has served that church for just over three years and is, according to those who know him best, a loving, caring person who has a heart for his people. He also has a heart for evangelism and makes every attempt to preach the whole gospel. In fact, some have complained that Tom is too evangelistic. Those most offended by Tom's zeal were Pete's parents, the Mullins.

Several months earlier the issue regarding Tom's evangelistic concerns came to a head at one of the church board meetings. Tom was introducing a plan for involving more church members in the task of evangelism when Bob Mullins, Pete's father, jumped to his feet: "Tom, I object to all of this. You are a good pastor. We know that you care for people. Our church is growing. More and more families are attending our services. Why put all of this in jeopardy with an evangelistic approach that will turn them off? Your God is too small. You need to soften your appeal to include those who might understand God differently. Surely the God of the Muslim is the same as the God of the Christian. What difference does it make just so long as we are sincere? Do what Jesus did. Preach sermons about everyday life. Let's feed the hungry bellies and let God tend to the soul." With that Bob sat down to mild applause, obviously pleased with himself. A few others made additional comments before the plan was tabled for further consideration.

Pete Mullins

Pete is just 17. He was raised in a "Christian" home and attended church regularly. In fact he was president of the youth fellowship. Tom and Pete had an extremely close relationship. Pete admired Tom and two years earlier had expressed a sincere desire to know God better. Tom had challenged him on a number of occasions to make Jesus Christ Lord of his life but Pete had kept putting it off saying: "In good time Tom, all in good time." Amy his girl friend had wanted to press the matter but had kept putting it off.

The Night of the Accident

Bob Mullins had called Tom to the hospital. When Tom arrived Bob and Shirley Mullins were warm and appreciative but then Bob added: "Go in there and see him, but if he should be conscious do not get too evangelistic. He does not know just how serious it is and you will scare him to death. Comfort him. He is already a Christian. Just let him know we love him and pray for him."

The Dilemma

Tom's mind is spinning. Pete's parents are concerned for Pete's comfort and support. Amy is concerned for his salvation. Tom is concerned for both. Pete no doubt feels helpless. He has no freedom. Tubes are running in and out of him. Tom thinks to himself: "What can I say? He probably won't even be conscious."

Just at that moment the doors to the ICU open. Tom walks into the room. He sees Pete. As he approaches the bed he hears the machines whirring. Suddenly Pete's eyes open. . . .

DISCUSSION GUIDE

This case has a number of facets. Even if the decision is made to say *something,* what should Tom say and how should he say it? What about Pete? What might he be feeling? How can Tom minister most effectively to him? If God does not intervene Pete will probably not live out the night. What can Tom realistically hope to accomplish in ten minutes? As pastor, what is Tom's responsibility to Pete. Should he take Pete's parents' advice? Should he take Amy's advice?

Questions to consider

1. What are the issues regarding Pete's relationship with God?

2. What is your advice to Tom regarding Pete, regarding his parents, and regarding Amy?
3. What would you do?
4. What is the role of the Holy Spirit in all of this?
5. What about the issue of healing?

Part II

Establishing a Sphere of Influence

Chapter 5
Messianic Complexes Die Hard

Evangelism is not a solo performance, it is a team accomplishment. It is the work, not of an individual, but of a fellowship. Every member of a church, and every organization and activity, should have a part in it. — *George Sweazey*

Recently I had to make a decision. On the same day, I received two different invitations to speak for the same period of time. Both invitations were asking me to speak on similar topics. The question was—which opportunity would be the better investment of time? Since all of us have to make similar decisions almost daily, Part II is especially important.

Part I sought to establish the core of the gospel—what we preach. Part II seeks to demonstrate the importance of knowing those persons to whom we minister most effectively—our sphere of influence. It has occurred to me that I reach only about 10% of the people whom I seek to influence. The other 90% will respond more easily to someone else. Frequently, in our eagerness to do all things well, we spend so much time among the 90% that we fail to minister effectively among the other 10%. True, the apostle Paul exhorts us to be "all things to all people." This does not mean, however, that we reach everyone we seek to win for Jesus Christ. Paul certainly did not. But it does mean that our spheres of influence represent a pretty good cross section of society. Consequently, our 10% is so diverse that it is sometimes difficult to identify. These next few chapters seek to assist us in making this identity clearer.

DEFINING ONE'S SPHERE OF INFLUENCE

Again, the major thesis of this book involves establishing the core of the gospel and then discovering where we can minister most effectively. This should accomplish two related objectives. First, it demonstrates that no one person alone can touch all the bases. No one body part can do it all. If you are the pastor of your church and if you are the only one doing ministry, then 90% of the people's needs are not being met. Total evangelism involves the total church, including all of her body parts. Second, it demonstrates that each of us is indispensable to the task. All of the body parts are vital to the minstry of evangelism. This chapter discusses the first of these two objectives. The second objective will be discussed in the chapter following.

Recently, my wife and I were traveling by plane back to Tulsa from Los Angeles. Seated next to me was a middle-aged businessman from New Zealand, and I sought to initiate a conversation. After a half-hour, I realized that I knew much about him, but that he knew practically nothing about me, and seemed uninterested in me. As I thought about this, I began to realize that the greatest gift I could give to this man for the rest of the journey was total silence. Although I had perhaps ministered to him in a way simply by listening to him, when I wanted to push on and "evangelize" I felt a check. Not that the situation was that difficult. It would have been relatively easy to shift the direction of "his" interests to "my" agenda. Quite frankly, God is so much a part of my life that it is easier to talk about Him than to talk about the weather. Nathan Marsh Pusey, former president of Harvard University, stated that the mark of an educated man is that he can talk about Jesus Christ without adolescent embarrassment. I like that. I could have talked about God with my traveling companion but it just did not feel right. I realized that he would not hear the gospel from me. Then I remembered. That morning I had asked God to make me especially sensitive to those opportunities for ministry. By the same token, however, I had also prayed that I would know when to keep silent. Ministry is multifaceted. Although we all have opportunity to evangelize, not all ministry is evangelism. Jesus established the precedent.

The life and ministry of Jesus demonstrates time and again the entire range of what it means to serve others. Jesus was not just a great evangelist. He was a superb teacher and healer as well. Although His ministry touched thousands of lives, His followers were relatively few. Only 120 remained faithful until Pentecost. So, what does this say to us?

If the ministry of Jesus is our pattern, then we, too, must

see evangelism within a larger perspective. Some will respond to our attempts to proclaim, while others will respond to our attempts to serve. Yet, no one person can do it all. Quite simply, our sphere of influence can be defined as those persons who respond most easily to our particular ministry. Without attempting here to establish who those people are, it is important to realize that they are the ones for whom God will hold us especially accountable. More will be said about this in the next two chapters. For now, however, we need to reemphasize the fact once again that we cannot reach everyone. Let me be more specific.

THE MESSIANIC COMPLEX

Many young Christians (especially within the evangelical wing of the church) fall prey to the belief that they must spend every moment evangelizing. Upon conversion, the sudden realization of what we have been missing is so strong that we carry a heavy burden for all the unsaved. This is as it should be. The problem is that if we do not see evangelism as a function of the entire church, we try to do it all ourselves. The result? We are frequently rejected and become easily discouraged. Jesus invites us to be selective. In Matthew 7, He says: "Do not give dogs what is sacred." We reply: "But I don't know any dogs. Surely one man's dog is another man's disciple." True, but the principle here is our need to be selective. For us to minister in some circles is simply to invite rejection. Again, let me illustrate.

When I was newly converted, I honestly tried to "save" everything that wiggled. I felt a special burden for preachers and seminary professors. I knew that I had the truth and was convinced that the whole world would listen. The cure for such arrogance was brutal. As you can imagine, I was not well received by some. The greater tragedy, however, was not that I was simply turned off, but that I sinned in the process. I became judgmental and condemnatory. I am certain that I did not serve Christ and His kingdom in many of those earlier encounters.

EVANGELISM: A FUNCTION OF THE ENTIRE BODY OF CHRIST

Messianic complexes fail to acknowledge the importance of

the other body parts. The verses, 1 Corinthians 12:12, 21, apply: "The body is a unit, though it is made up of many parts; and though all its parts are many, they form one body. . . . The eye cannot say to the hand, 'I don't need you!' and the head cannot say to the feet, 'I don't need you!'" If I am attempting to do it all, then I am not trusting your ability to function in the body. We are different parts. Our differences (which all too often divide us) should unite and strengthen us.

During my last two years as a professor at Fuller Seminary in Pasadena, California, I refused to accept any speaking assignments in Southern California if I could not bring six students with me. We were a team and we functioned as such. On my own, it would not be unusual for me to have ten to twelve hours center stage during a weekend. With six students along, however, I was fortunate to have twenty minutes center stage. The result? I found that I could be just as effective in twenty minutes with my team as I could with ten to twelve hours on my own. Not only did we function as individuals, but our individual ministries complemented one another so that we were *all* more effective. Truly, the whole is greater than the sum of its parts. Such is the economy of God.

The point is that our sphere is big, but not so big that we cannot trust the other body parts to pick up where one leaves off. Similarly, our spheres are small, but not so small that we can lose our vision for our own responsibility.

UNITY, NOT UNIFORMITY

That part of our gospel presentation that is not absolutely essential to salvation has been called "baggage." We have already established that it is this baggage that helps to create our spheres of influence. Our messianic complexes die when we realize that we are limited in our appeal. That is not to stifle our vision; it is simply to acknowledge the importance of and our dependence upon the other body parts. Again, no one person can do it all. Our baggage marks our uniqueness. Everyone is unique. If we are faithful to ourselves (i.e., we do not try to be someone else), we soon realize that this gives us an edge in some circles. We are different. *Unity, however, does not imply uniformity*. It is hoped we are together on the core, but this should not lead us to believe that our presentations must be similar as well. In fact, *true unity implies diversity.* Together, different body parts form the whole. This morning I looked at my daughter saying to myself: "My, she is so pretty." Then I realized that she would not be nearly so pretty if she were all ear. She would be even less pretty if she were all mouth. No, in order to be who she is she needs all of her body parts. That is a powerful image. It frees us; yet it holds us accountable. Such accountability provides the thrust for the following chapter.

We conclude this chapter where we began. The answer to the question as to which invitation to accept came in the replies to some inquiries that I wrote to both churches. First, what do you feel that I have to offer? Second, what are the pressing needs? And finally, do they submit to my particular strengths? On the surface, these questions might seem presumptuous, but I have found that if the invitation has been extended prayerfully, few take offense and our time together is given a far greater chance of success. The watchword for the eighteenth-century Evangelical Revival was "redeem the time." Surely, God will honor our attempts to choose our opportunities for ministry wisely. We are not the messiah. We cannot do it all. I know that is a difficult lesson for some of us to learn but, trust me, it is worth the effort.

Chapter 6
I'm Indispensable

Evangelism is making certain that new Christians are properly attached to the body of Christ.

Please read the following verses carefully. God probably had you in mind when Paul wrote them: "Now the body is not made up of one part, but of many. If the foot should say, 'Because I am not a hand, I do not belong to the body,' it would not for that reason cease to be a part of the body. And if the ear should say, 'Because I am not an eye, I do not belong to the body,' it would not for that reason cease to be a part of the body" (1 Cor. 12:14–16). God give us balance! If we do not have messianic complexes (believing that we can do all things), many of us have so little self-esteem that we think we can do nothing. Why do so many parts of the body race at breakneck speed, either to one extreme or the other? Let us look more closely at the passage quoted above.

ON BEING TRUE TO ONESELF

When I was a young Christian, I frequently admired the gifts of others. Many years ago I preached my first sermon in a downtown mission in Wheaton, Illinois. I remember the pride I felt when someone told me that I sounded just like Billy Graham. I do not know why I thought that was such a compliment, when my preaching did not get the kind of response Mr. Graham is accustomed to getting. The truth of the matter is that I was probably just as interested in exhibiting someone else's gifts as I was at getting a positive response to the gospel. God forgave me and I learned a valuable lesson. Many of us believe that if we do not have someone else's gift, we are no longer a part of the body. Not so!

The passage quoted denies that logic. Read a part of it again.

"If the foot should say, 'Because I am not a hand, I do not belong to the body,' it would not for that reason cease to be a part of the body." Many of us find ourselves saying: "I do not have this person's gift or that person's gift; so therefore I am no longer a part of the body." The rest of the body's parts should not allow you to get away with that. Every Christian has gifts. Of that you can be sure. If by some quirk it fulfills some need in your life to deny your own precious gifts, then so be it. But I, as a part of that same body, object. You can deny your gifts until the kingdom comes, but that does not make you any less a part of the body of Christ. Again, if you insist on hanging limp on the body of Christ, then so be it, but I object. You are for that reason no less a part of the body of Christ. Once you buy into the body of Christ by virtue of His grace, released by your faith in Him, then you are indispensable to it. The passage below follows the passage quoted above. Again, read it carefully.

> The eye cannot say to the hand, "I don't need you!" And the head cannot say to the feet, "I don't need you!" On the contrary, those parts of the body that seem to be weaker are indispensable, and the parts that we think are less honorable we treat with special honor. And the parts that are unpresentable are treated with special modesty, while our presentable parts need no special treatment. But God has combined the members of the body and has given greater honor to the parts that lacked it, so that there should be no division in the body, but that its parts should have equal concern for each other (1 Cor. 12:21–25).

The point should be fairly obvious. No matter how weak or incapable we feel for ministry, we are indispensable to it. The body cannot function at peak without our involvement. You come into contact with people every day who can respond most easily to you. Believe it! Act upon it! I may not have the gifts of a great evangelist, but no one can minister more effectively in my sphere than I can. No one can minister more effectively in your sphere than you can. Let me illustrate.

A man (we will call him Phillip) was a member of a small group that I was in for almost a year. We had been praying for a friend of his for some months, and Phillip had been trying to evangelize his friend for years. One day, as he described his friend's problem, I remember feeling that my own experience might gain me a hearing. We set up an appointment. The result? Phillip's friend made a commitment to Jesus Christ and has been moving ahead ever since. Now, do not misunderstand me. The response of Phillip's friend to my presentation does not mean that I did it all. Obviously not. It does mean that for those moments, Phillip's friend was in my sphere of influence and took another step toward giving his life to God—in this instance, the crucial step, although many steps would follow. Nor does this mean that just because someone is in our particular sphere he or she will necessarily receive Christ on the spot.

Recently I sat down next to a young man on an airplane. He wore a ring in his ear and when I asked him about it he quickly volunteered that he was gay. He began telling me about his life. For ten years he had been into witchcraft. When I asked why, he said that was the only religion that would accept him as a homosexual. I told him that he was wrong. I was a Christian, and although I could not condone his homosexuality, I could accept him for what he was. We talked on for the remainder of the trip. As we were parting, I said to him, "I know that you are into witchcraft right now, but I promise you that any philosophy built on revenge and superstition will one day let you down. If you ever reach the point where you want to say more about your life than "I'm gay," call me collect." I gave him my number and we parted. I honestly believed that he, too, was in my sphere of influence. He obviously did not accept Christ, but down the road another body part might well pick up where I left off. In the meantime I am praying that he calls. Quite frankly, I will be surprised if he does not.

ON BEING TRUE TO THE WHOLE

This same lesson has another side. Whereas I cannot be true to the whole without being true to myself, I cannot be true to myself without being true to the whole. I have gifts. I must not deny them. On the other hand, I must see their role in the body. I can be content with my gifts only if I know that other body parts can function adequately where I fall short. As seen previously, the passage that exhorts us to acknowledge our own indispensability also encourages us to appreciate the other body parts and our dependence upon them. We are indispensable *to one another.* Again, let me illustrate. Several years ago I read a book by the reknowned anthropologist, Richard Leaky, entitled *People of the Lake.* One of his discoveries especially intrigued me. The theory went something like this. Several million years ago four strains of man were apparently evolving simultaneously. Only one, however (homo sapien), survived to become modern man. The other three became extinct. Previously, the theory had been that only the "fittest" survived. Darwin stated that case in some detail. Leaky, however, discovered that it was not the fittest that survived. The fittest (what I call "macho" strains) were loners. Although they exhibited superior strength (they were forever running around beating their breast), they got singled out and picked off. Homo sapien was the only strain to survive, not because it was the strongest, but because it was the only strain *that dared to become community.*

We are important not only to our own particular sphere, but also to the whole. I am not subscribing to the weakest link theory. The Holy Spirit is constantly taking up slack. He will sometimes make the adjustment necessary to keep the body functioning in spite of its weakest member. The fact remains, however, that ministry was intended for the body. God delights in using His creation. He has chosen us. He has chosen you! If you are an ear, listen carefully. If you are a leg, walk straight. If you are an eye, watch closely. *Together,* we can storm the very gates of hell. You cannot do it all, but you really are indispensable.

Chapter 7
Developing Personal Guidelines

Evangelism is often hindered in the church today, not through the laziness of Christians, but through the busyness of Christians in the wrong direction.
David Watson

I have frequently thought that Jesus never had to go out of His way to help anyone. He never had time. He was so sensitive to the needs directly in front of Him that they alone demanded all that He could give—and more!

We, too, can become sensitive to our opportunities for ministry directly in our path. Our spheres of influence rarely take us far afield. So, how do we recognize those spheres? This chapter corresponds to chapter 3, where we sought to establish guidelines for the core of the gospel. Here too we will begin with the rationale, bring a word of caution, briefly state a test sphere as a model, and then describe the guidelines used in that model.

THE RATIONALE FOR ESTABLISHING GUIDELINES

Thus far our primary suppositions could be restated as follows: 1) once the gospel message is clearly understood, we can seek to find an audience that will respond to our particular understanding. 2) Not only our understanding, but who, where, and what we are also affects who our audience might be. 3) We all have a sphere. We all have gifts. Although no one body part can do it all we are all indispensable. *Your* best may not be *the* best but it is all that God requires. If I am an ear, who needs someone to listen? If I am an eye, who needs someone to see? Whatever my sphere, whatever my gifts, someone out there needs me.

What all of this boils down to is this. Since I cannot do it all, do I seek to acknowledge and then sharpen my particular gifts so that I can see at least some results, or do I persist in stumbling along, experiencing so much rejection that I tend to burn out all together? I have come to realize that twenty minutes in my sphere can be more fruitful than three or four hours in someone else's. If I can see my own peculiarities as strengths, I find I do not have to apologize for who I am. Within my sphere I can be myself. Outside my sphere, I often attempt to be someone else. Within my sphere, I can speak out of my own experience. Outside, I often resort to someone else's. Within my sphere, I can relax. Outside, I am uneasy and anxious. Within my sphere, the right words come more easily at the right time. Outside, finding the right word at the right time is frequently like trying to dredge up dusty facts on the Medes and the Persians.

A WORD OF CAUTION

As with the core, establishing guidelines for the sphere of influence needs some added perspective. Again, guidelines are just that, no more, no less. They do not imply a tight system. Since our spheres tend to change with each new experience, we need to be open and flexible enough to allow for shifts (although frequently subtle) in direction. The tighter the system, the slower the learner. I like what Isaiah 42:10 says about a "new song." Guidelines are not to inhibit us. If our system is too tight, we find it difficult to learn anything new because each new thought tends to affect the whole. God is always teaching us new songs.

Recently I read an article about the various kinds of mathematics that have divided the scientific world. There is no longer an absolute math. In our five-dimensional universe, 2 + 2 = 4. That just might not be true in the sixth dimension. We tend to see logic in a straight line—cause and effect. Our spheres of influence have so many variables, however, that they rarely submit to straight-line logic. The caution is to develop the kinds of guidelines that leave some room for mystery—the word from on high—the work of the Holy Spirit.

One final word of caution has to do with the word "relational" itself. Some of us, quite frankly, do not see ourselves as relational. That, however, is not the issue here. Relational does not intend to imply that we must be outgoing or gregarious. It means a *ministry in relationships.* Certainly all of us do not relate easily in some situations. That, however, is precisely the point. Although we do not relate easily, let us say socially, for example, we all have relationships. Those relationships provide us with our opportunity to evangelize. Thus, being sensitized to those who can respond to our particular gifts is what this chapter is all about. With this clearly in mind, let me model this exercise by first briefly stating a segment of my own sphere and then describing the guidelines I used in establishing it.

A TEST SPHERE STATED

It seems to me that if this chapter is to make sense I must provide some kind of a model. Since we best speak with authority out of our own experience, let me state a part of my own sphere as I understand it now.

My sphere (as stated earlier) includes those who respond most easily to my ministry. Let us assume for a moment that by "ministry" we do not mean those casual kinds of "one-shot" encounters where there is little opportunity for follow-up. Although these brief encounters are subject to the same guidelines, for our purposes here let us refer only to that ministry that has at least some potential for long-term testing and evaluation.

I am the son of a son of a minister. Although I was a pastor for nearly twelve years, I have spent a good many years in the academic environment. Commitment and congruency are important to me. I have experienced a great deal of both joy and pain. I enjoy running, skiing, and chess. With this brief description as grist for a segment of my sphere, who reponds most easily to me? Let me illustrate with some particulars.

At the present I am discipling six of my students. At the beginning of the semester, the word gets around that I am willing to disciple several students who will submit to a prescribed discipline. After brief interviews six are chosen. Although the precise meaning of "discipling" will surface in later chapters, let it suffice for now to say that I meet with each of these students individually each week. The purpose of our meeting together is to hold them accountable for their spiritual development. They set the agenda, not I. They trust me sufficiently to reveal areas of needed growth, and we discuss these areas each week. Again, they set the agenda. That means I do not have to say where *I* feel they are falling short. Our relationship is such that they feel free enough to confess openly the real and potential barriers to true spirituality. Since these students seek me out, a brief word about them personally should reveal something of my sphere of influence.

One of these students is an older man who spent several years in the business world before coming to seminary. Another is a messianic Jew who came to seminary after six months alone in the California desert. Another is a young man raised on a Wisconsin dairy farm who plans to transfer to a seminary within his own denomination at the end of this academic year. Another is an undergraduate student planning on medical school in the fall. Another is a man from the midwest who came to seminary from a large family that is only partially in sympathy with his plans for the ordained ministry. The last is a Texan, anxiously looking for the niche that is (to use his words) larger than baseball, hot dogs, apple pie—and yes, even Texas.

As I considered these persons, several characteristics seemed to emerge out of so much apparent diversity. They were all relatively young—twenty to thirty-three. They are all men. Although two are uncertain as to what form their ministry will take, they are deeply committed to Christ and His church. They are all unsatisfied with their present level of spirituality and sense the need for help, especially in the area of discipline. Five are single (although one is engaged) and one is married, with four children. All are open, teachable, and receive advice without complaint. None is bound too tightly by any one theological system, although all are biblically oriented and are searching for theological insights to instruct them in their various kinds of spiritual experiences.

As I consider this brief sketch, several insights begin to surface about my own sphere of influence. Again, this is not an absolute. I always try to be sensitive to the Holy Spirit who occasionally leads me to the inevitable exception. This, however, is what I have discovered. Generally speaking, I work most effectively with younger men who are receptive to my own attempts at commitment, congruency, and openness. I am certain that my own evangelical/charismatic stance (though not necessarily in the classical mold) also contributes to my sphere. I find several other common areas as well. I have a penchant for biblical truths (though not in the fundamental scholastic sense); so do they. I appreciate tough theological reflection; so do they. I insist upon a reasonable amount of discipline of body/mind/spirit; so do they, although we all struggle in these areas at times and openly confess our need for improvement. They all seek a fresh encounter with God. I frequently exhort them to be so open to truth, from whatever source, that they can experience some kind of spiritual/emotional/intellectual breakthrough at least once a week. Ergo, having said this, several variables arise as well.

Raw intelligence does not seem to play an important role. Some of these students are clearly more intelligent than others. Theological background does not seem to matter. Some come out of a more classical denominational mold; some do not. Some are fairly sophisticated theologically; some are not. My own theological training does not seem to matter much, at least as to its direction. Although most are fairly compatible theologically, some are pretty far apart on some fairly basic issues. I seem to have their respect and trust, but none stands particularly in awe. We are comfortable with mutual exchange. Give-and-take is placed at a premium. So, although this is only a segment of my so-called sphere of influence, I feel that it is substantial enough to demonstrate our method. Now, what criteria did I use to establish such a sphere? These criteria will comprise the guidelines to follow.

GUIDELINES

In describing my own sphere of influence, certain criteria were used in making such a judgment. Obviously, we began with my own experience. Several students, in effect, identified themselves as a part of my sphere. Although this was not an evangelistic setting as such, the same rules applied. Along with experience, however, several other factors (personality, proximity, commonality, and the role of the Spirit) surfaced as well. All of these will be included under the above heading of "Guidelines."

Experience

My own experience teaches me much about my sphere of influence. Who, out there, responds to me? What kind of people seek me out? Are there any common denominators? Is there a discernable pattern? In most cases I think there is. We've noticed that in my own experience a definite pattern emerges that should alert me to those future opportunities for ministry. Let's break this down.

First of all, once I am available and am willing to minister, what kind of people move toward me? Who responds to my "call"? Who feels comfortable around me? With whom do I feel comfortable sharing my feelings? With whom do I share my failures as well as my successes? Is there anyone with whom I can cry? Who feels free to cry with me? Whom can I call at 4:00 A.M.? Whose names do I remember and use when greeting them? Who knows that I listen to them? Who senses that I have compassion and empathy for them? Who knows that I will keep their personal feelings and experiences absolutely confidential? As you can see, the list of questions could go on indefinitely. The point is that many people within our proximity need ministry desperately. Which ones belong to us? Someone once told me that he would move as close to me as I was willing to move toward him. I think that comment stayed with me because it packs a larger truth. Much of the world is waiting to be touched by me.

Second, to whom do I move toward? What burden has been imposed upon my heart? For whom do I pray? What issues do I discuss with other Christians? As I move through the day, representing the body of Jesus Christ, do I possess a certain knowledge in a field by way of language, ways of thinking, special interest, or other means of relating that seem specialized and not readily interchangeable with other patterns? Is God-talk natural to me? With whom do I share the gospel most easily?

Personality

Again, it would not do to overstate my case here, but certain personality traits are important. Most people will not share intimately with someone they do not perceive as trustworthy, genuinely concerned, and able to help. I find that trust and respect usually surface out of commitment and congruency. By commitment, I meant commitment to Jesus Christ. By congruency I means it is important to look the same on the outside as we do on the inside. If we are a triangle on the inside, we must look like a triangle on the outside. Too often our testimony lacks the ring of truth because our words do not seem to run deep enough into our own experience. For example, genuine piety is genuine because it rarely draws attention to itself. Many of us are suspicious of the kind of piety that looks pious only in contrast to impiety. Genuine piety simply creates a quality of personhood that we want to emulate. Certainly all of these traits figure prominently in our sphere of influence.

Proximity

We cannot minister to people unless we come into contact with them. On the surface that might not seem helpful, but the issue has a more subtle side. Many of us, for example, do not realize that our proximity with some includes ministry within our workaday world. It is not enough to say that our proximity includes the block on which we live, or even our hometown. More specifically, our proximity is where we move comfortably on that block or in that town. Every day, within the normal course of events, working, shopping, or running errands, many opportunities occur for ministry. In a recent book by Howard Figler entitled the *Complete Job Search Book,* he comments regarding the context necessary for some of us to find work: "Your best connections are the ones you trip over every day, the people who cross your path on a natural routine basis. They may not have the keys to the executive washroom, but they inevitably know people who do and can introduce you in casual context. . . . Personal contacts are neighbors, friends, colleagues, relatives, teachers, supervisors. Our lives are full of potential personal contacts. We all know someone. The trick is to see it that way." The relevance of that statement for relational evangelism seems to me to be fairly obvious. The "contacts," our opportunities for ministry, are all around us. This raises still another issue to which we have already alluded. Do I make myself available? In fact, do I want to minister? A student declared in a paper, written on this very topic, the following: "It would be pointless to work up some hypothetical sphere of influence when, in fact, I am not certain that I want to influence anyone." We must not only be there, we must be willing to minister at the supermarket, the cleaners, the garage. Every day is packed with potential for those who are sensitive.

To state the same case a bit differently, one might well ask, In what specific ministry within the church structure have I been involved, or am currently involved, or am getting involved? Related questions include, Why has a change taken place in my present ministry? Do I feel comfortable with any new direction? Are the results more fulfilling and satisfying?

Commonality

Common experience can easily help to establish a person's sphere. Common goals, common joys or common pains, common enemies, even common theological perspectives can all serve to create the kind of bond that is conducive to ministry. Occasionally a relationship will be engendered through a candid disclosure of some struggle or problem on one person's part that is common to the other. This aspect of ministry will be discussed in some detail in later chapters. For now, whether the relationship begins with the sharing of a struggle or a problem or these come up as a later development of the relationship, the sharing of common struggles will tend to solidify the relationship. It is important to remember, however, that to serve as a basis for relational evangelism, the struggles in the Christian life do not all have to be resolved. We may still be struggling with some problem. This does not mean that we should hide them. In fact, they may be the key to winning our friend to Christ.

Common goals have also brought people together. Our own country was torn by civil strife, and continuing division and factions persisted until they were welded together against the common enemy in World War I.

I stated that in my own experience theological perspective did not seem so vital (which might say as much about me as it does about anyone else), but in a theological setting such as a seminary, this is bound to have some bearing. I find that those responding to me are at least *open* to my interpretation of the gospel core.

The Holy Spirit

Perhaps this is where we should have begun. Ultimately the Holy Spirit is the great evangel. No matter how well-suited a particular person might be to our sphere of influence, the Holy Spirit must open the door nonetheless.

Likewise, we must always be open for the Holy Spirit to direct us, even to someone outside our normal sphere. After all, God is sovereign, and occasionally He will work in ways that are foreign to our own understanding. Chapter 15 will deal with this almost exclusively.

A GENTLE REMINDER

At this point is might be good to conclude with still another word of caution. Please, do not use these guidelines as you might a yardstick. Do not measure people as if by the end of your thumb. These guidelines are not a checklist. They should become a part of the warp and woof of our own mind and spirit so that they become second nature. Simply to be aware of them enters those data into the computer so that we begin to develop a *feel* for ministry.

Similarly, not all of the guidelines need apply. Two or three of them could well be sufficient. You will need to develop a sensitivity for this as your ministry matures. It is also important to remember that these are *my* guidelines. Just as with the core, they are not necessarily yours. These guidelines are not to do your work for you. This exercise fails in its primary objective if you are not challenged as well as encouraged to do your own reflection. Remember, relational evangelism must relate to *your* experience.

Chapter 8
A Case Study

The following case study (like the one in chapter 4) has been designed as a teaching aid. This case attempts to demonstrate the importance of establishing one's sphere of influence.

THE CASE: ED'S DILEMMA

Ed Keating sat alone on the couch, silently praying. He was depressed for no apparent reason. Everything in his life seemed to be going so well. He thought to himself that being down when he should have been up served only to increase his depression. His wife, Nancy, was just putting the finishing touches on a meal for themselves and Marilee, an employee at the supermarket Ed managed. Since Marilee knew that Ed had spent some time studying in a theological seminary, she had expressed an interest in Christianity. Ed had invited her over to talk about it. This would be a great opportunity to witness. So, why was he down? He decided it was because he had no idea what to say. Although he had been a Christian for a number of years and had memorized several gospel presentations, he had never led anyone to Christ. He was questioning his own commitment. Why had he never led anyone to faith? Was it because of sin in his life? These and other unanswered questions had prompted an earlier decision to leave seminary and to discontinue his pursuit of the ordained ministry. As he sat waiting for Marilee, he was not only praying for the right words, but he was asking God whether or not he should say anything at all.

Perhaps a silent witness was best for him. On the other hand, Marilee had opened the door—she had approached him. Maybe this was a sign that he should once again be bold. If he could just lead one person to Christ, he might even return to seminary.

Background

At the beginning of his sophomore year in high school, Ed first understood the claims of Christ on his life. Before this time, he had had more faith in his ability to play golf than in God. Even though he was a "scratch" player, however, and had for some time considered a career as a pro, he had found this lifestyle to be self-defeating and empty. Then, in the process of taking communion on a church retreat, he had come face to face with the fact of Christ's death and resurrection, and His love for him. He responded by giving as much as he knew of himself to as much as he knew of God. From that day forward, he had participated in some form of ministry, usually as a leader.

Within a year of that first experience, Ed had become involved in establishing a club for Christians in his high school. As a part of the leadership, he frequently lead the singing, brought his friends, attended Bible studies, and shared his faith openly. The club flourished, but its success did not appear to be contingent on his efforts. About this time, Ed's church had begun a lay evangelism program, and he saw this as an opportunity to be trained in-depth. The style of evangelism they practiced was to knock on the doors of those who had visited his church and to present the gospel as briefly and simply as possible. Frequently the invitation amounted to, "there it is, take it or leave it." Ed finished the training part of the course and began visitation with a team of experienced church members. Again, although people seemed to be helped somewhat he witnessed no changed lives, and as far as he was concerned, if "take it or leave it" was the only approach to evangelism, he, too, would leave it. Soon after this, Ed graduated from high school and went away to college.

The first half of his college years was spent as an active member of an evangelistic group of Christians on campus. He received fellowship from this body of believers, and was trained to share his faith by means of a prescribed formula.

Again, he accompanied the leaders on some of their appointments. He even did some visitation on his own, but with still no apparent results. By this time he began to be defensive about the subject of evangelism, and gradually withdrew from this particular group. Not long afterward, Ed found himself in still another youth-type ministry. Here, his energies were directed into a club of boys, ages 10–15, in a housing project for blacks. This work was primarily focused on meeting social needs, but also included weekly object lessons that portrayed biblical truths. This work seemed to be more suited to his gifts, whatever they were. Unfortunately, Ed seemed to fail at bridging the cultural and ethnic gap that existed. So, another apparent failure haunted him—perhaps he just needed more training. And it was at this time that Ed decided to attend seminary. His last year of college was spent working to save money, as well as in studying.

Soon after college Ed married Nancy. They quickly moved to Michigan to attend an evangelical seminary. During his first year in seminary, Ed was active once again in organizing an evangelical youth group. Unfortunately, he was unable to do the necessary contact work because of the pressure of school. This time when his ministry proved once again to be fruitless in terms of personal evangelism he felt that he had the answer. It was because he lacked commitment. So, his past failures, his lack of commitment, but primarily his inability to lead someone else to Christ, haunted him.

In Ed's second year of seminary, he and Nancy participated in a lay renewal team that ministered to churches. A six-member team would lead a congregation through a series of training sessions and small group experiences. Through them, church members learned to express their spiritual needs and to pray for one another. This was by far Ed's most meaningful ministry experience up to this point. Yet, he was seriously questioning his call to full-time Christian work. Eventually he decided to leave the seminary and enter the business world. He moved back to his home town and took a position with a small grocery firm.

Marilee

Ed first met Marilee when she came seeking a job at one of the stores he managed. They became close friends shortly after she was hired.During the following year they shared in many thought-provoking discussions and learned to respect each other's opinions. As their trust for each other grew, so did their candor, and before long, Ed began to talk about his relationship with Jesus Christ.

One day Marilee, a senior in high school, asked Ed if he would read and make a critique of her English term theme. The paper was to be a treatise on her philosophy of life—existentialism. Ed read the paper carefully and suggested to her that they discuss it. This was a perfect opportunity to explain his own philosophy of life. He shared with Marilee his experience in seminary and much to his surprise, she expressed a real interest in Christianity. So, Ed and Nancy had invited Marilee over for dinner in order to discuss it.

The Dilemma

Ed had always felt a call to full-time Christian service. Although he was a success in his position with the grocery firm, he was still unsatisfied. Even though he felt he was unable to express his faith adequately to others, that same faith was working for himself. Many of their friends seemed miserable, but Ed and Nancy were happy. How could he best bring their friends to faith in Jesus Christ? He believed Christ to be the answer. So, as he sat praying on the couch, anticipating Marilee's arrival, all of the old doubts began to haunt him once again.

At that point the doorbell rang. Rather than go to the door himself he said: "Nancy, would you please get the door? I'm going out back and turn the steaks." As Ed stood staring into the coals of the fire he thought to himself once again: "What should I do, Lord? Should I say nothing? Should I be bold?" At that moment Nancy followed Marilee onto the patio where Ed was standing. Marilee extended her hand toward Ed and said: "Ed, it's so nice of you to have me over. . . ."

DISCUSSION GUIDE

This case focuses on Ed Keating's sphere of influence. Admittedly, the issues could be complex. What is his sphere of influence? How can he minister most effectively within it? Finally, how can he best prepare for such a ministry?

Questions to Consider

1. What is your advice to Ed Keating? Should he be bold and speak out to Marilee?
2. What about his life's work? In your opinion should he remain as the manager of the grocery firm, or should he consider returning to seminary?
3. What would you say to Ed about evangelism? What advice could you give to him that might help him to see the joy of sharing one's faith in a larger perspective?

CONCLUSION

Although the names have been changed, the information for this case was given to me by Charles Halley a former student of mine at Fuller Theological Seminary. Charlie shared his faith with the young high-school girl. The result? Six weeks later, Marilee prayed with Charlie and received Jesus Christ as her personal Savior. Charlie returned to seminary and is now pastoring a church.

Part III

Meeting Felt Needs

Chapter 9
The Needy People

Evangelism is one beggar telling another beggar where to find bread. D. T. Niles

I don't want to sound too mundane, but it has occurred to me that evangelism, per se, like most things, works on the principle of supply and demand. If there is a big enough need, then some enterprising person will offer the supply. Where evangelism is concerned, we obviously do not realize just how big the need is. Engel and Norton, in their book, *What's Gone Wrong With the Harvest?*, inform us that in an age when the mass media span the globe, when literacy is growing rapidly, and when people in many quarters are showing new interest in spiritual things, we still have not penetrated world society with the fundamental truths of the Good News. Nor do we understand just how monumental the task is . Leighton Ford, in his book, *One Way to Change the World,* tells us that it takes an average of 1,000 Christians working 365 days a year, to win one convert for Jesus Christ. Small wonder the entire body of Christ is called to evangelize.

A few months ago I flew over the bridge that spans Tampa Bay. I was reminded that this was the same bridge that was struck by a tanker in a dense fog causing the roadway to collapse so that a number of drivers drove right off the edge to their deaths. Someone finally pulled off a shirt and started to flag down traffic. That said something to me as to how the world will look after its own. Should we not have the same sense of urgency. If supply and demand applies here, perhaps we need to be reminded just how considerable the need is. Bridges are out all over the world.

LORD, I NEED HELP

Many Christians view the world as fairly oblivious to its needs, at least from the Christian perspective. That may be true to an extent, but the world is certainly not oblivious to the kinds of needs to which the gospel offers an answer. Let me illustrate.

I mentioned earlier that most people "out there" do not like doing what they do. Work offers little more than work. It is a job, necessary to them only because it puts the roof over their head and bread on the table. For the most part life is a bit of a drag, to be endured only between weekend bashes. The cocktail party promises more relief than the worship service in some neighborhood church. We Americans still attend church at a rate of less than 40 percent. We say to ourselves, "At least the 'spirits' in the local bar produce what they promise." We are conditioned to be entertained. Too much of what we experience in the local church is not only not entertaining, it is not even religious. I once served as a chaplain for a professional football team. I spoke to them on Sunday morning before the game. I remember on one such occasion, a young man coming to me and saying, "Listen, preacher, do not feel that you have to talk to us about football; talk to us about Jesus—I am twenty-five years old and my career is heading downhill, and you had better help me put this darn thing in perspective." God, in an age when people are desperately in need, deliver us from Sunday morning fluff. If supply is determined by demand, then truly the demand is great.

Even more to the point is the fact that most people "out there" not only dislike their work, they dislike themselves. Psychologists are beginning to say that emotional illness results, not so much from suppressing inherent desire (sex and aggression) as from suppressing basic reality (love and truth), so that we no longer like ourselves and our subconscious minds are forever bailing out into some kind of morbid fantasy. Again, if supply is determined by demand, then truly the demand is great. My friend, evangelist Jack Gray, says: "Misery is God's number one evangelistic weapon." Think about it.

Christopher Lach's book, *Narcissism,* attempts to summerize the prevailing value system in terms of "ins" and "outs." The permissive society is in; guilt and punishment are out. Self-help is in; authority is out. Leisure is in; working is out. Spending is in; saving is out. Selling yourself and role play are in; craftsmanship is out. Therapy is in; religion is out. Superficiality is in; depth is out. Nonbinding relationships are in; commitments are out. In a phrase, the present values are epitomized by the rock world and Hollywood—a narcissiastic culture. Jim Laney, president of Emory University, calls this an age of "herpes, heroin, and homeless children." If supply is determined by demand, then truly the demand is great. Again, the point here is that the world may not identify its needs as spiritual, but it can certainly identify a need. What better way to evangelize than to begin with a *felt need.* Nothing is more difficult than trying to convince some people of sin—of their need for God. Oh, we will happily knock on their doors if the house is on fire but we are hesitant to warn them of sin in their lives. Our task, therefore, is frequently to establish a relationship out of which needs can surface, and then seek to apply the gospel truth to meet those needs. Sometimes the house is on fire and they do not even realize it. More will be said about the mechanics of that in the next chapter. Let it suffice for now to say that it is first of all important to realize that the need is great so that the supply can be even greater.

HOW CHRISTIANS VIEW THE WORLD

Our style of ministry is largely determined by how we view the world. We seek to supply an answer for whatever problem we perceive to be at hand. Like it or not, the world sets the agenda, at least initially. Otherwise, we are answering questions that have not been asked. Just for a moment, stop and ask yourself how you view the world. Then ask someone else. You might even ask a Christian, and then a non-Christian. Make a list. Let me illustrate.

Frequently I ask my students to describe their view of the world. The point is that we view ministry in terms of need. Billy Graham sees the world as lost. His message is salvation. Oral Roberts sees the world as sick. His message is healing. Jesse Jackson sees the world as oppressed. His message is freedom. Robert Schuller sees the world as suffering from low self-esteem. His message is that you are precious and important. To add to this, here are a few categories expressed by my students. One class views the world as spiritually needy, searching for meaning and reality, hurting out of some disappointed relationship, emotionally broken, lonely, separated, hypocritical, masked, pretending, sinful, in bondage to fear, disparing, helpless, needing a touch from God, unable to believe that God is a good God. Obviously, this says a great deal about how they will seek to minister. Personally, I see the world as plagued by broken relationships. People are out of orbit with God, themselves, and those around them. Consequently, I see ministry in terms of reconciliation. I fully intend to spend the rest of my life helping people feel better about God, themselves, and those around them.

WHAT CAN SUCH A NEEDY WORLD TEACH ME?

Teach me, world, that I may care. The fact that the world is needy should not create in us an air of self-righteousness. We need to assess needs realistically, but we must resist becoming "holier than thou." The world has much to teach us about life. I find it extremely difficult to learn from those who wish to pit their wisdom against my ignorance. I would much rather that these people put their knowledge with my knowledge, that we might arrive at a higher knowledge together. All too often we react rather than respond, as if to confront the world with *our* agenda, only to find that the world has an agenda of its own. *People are never the enemy. Sin is the enemy.* Sensitivity and patience are obviously important. Sometimes a little creativity will allow an opportunity to surface. Let me illustrate.

My niece, Tempe, is a sophomore in college. Over a Christmas break, she was invited to a party where most of the activity focused on "smoking dope." Tempe sat down and was soon joined by another girl who asked, "Do you have a light?" Tempe replied, "Yes, I do. He lives in me twenty-four hours a day. His name is Jesus, and you can use Him any old time you please. Would you like to hear about Him?" Believe it or not, the girl did.

Soon Tempe and her new friend were joined by still another girl who commented, "You guys are talking about Jesus. I'd like to know more." Tempe replied, "What do you know already?" And so it went throughout the night. These girls became happily absorbed in exchanging their ideas about Jesus Christ. That is the way it happened. Who would have thought that Jesus would have received such a welcome in that environment?

John Wesley once thought it nearly a sin to convert anyone outside the church, yet his ministry was sustained by taking his message, quite literally, *to the world.* Gordon Causby, at the Church of the Savior in Washington, D. C., makes the point that we need not necessarily bring people to the church in order to introduce them to Jesus Christ. We might just as effectively go into the world and bear witness to the Christ who is already at work in the world. That, of course, is the story of prevenient grace. Prevenient grace describes the Spirit of the Lord calling us before we were born, who from our birth has made mention of our name (Isa. 49:1; cf. Ps. 22:9–10). It describes the Spirit who gently moves our wills, who draws and woos us, as it were, to walk in the light. It describes the "hound of heaven" stalking, if not courting us, between conception and conversion, preventing us from moving so far from the way that when we finally understand the claims of the gospel on our lives, He guarantees our freedom to say yes. So, God is already preparing the way for our evangelistic task. For example, the Spirit sent Philip to the Ethiopian eunuch, but by the time he arrived, the stage had already been set, as the man was already reading the Scriptures. When Peter got to Cornelius, most of the work had been done. In fact, Paul's conversion is an example of where the Spirit of Christ did it all by Himself.

The world has needs. Of that you can be sure. The world might not interpret its needs as spritual, but you can well believe that the world knows it is in trouble. Christians have to be aware of the needs of the world. We can learn from them. We need not be intimidated by them or fear them. We have a great and good God who is already at work in the world and He is going to change that world. Who knows, perhaps that promise is already being fulfilled? Let's you and me get in on the fun! God's prevenient grace is at work everywhere and in everyone. Let's get our shirts off and start flagging down traffic because the bridges are out all over the world.

Chapter 10
Allowing Needs to Surface

Evangelism is love in the eye of the believer.

Approaches to evangelism have been compared with extracting a chick from its shell. It can be done with a hammer or it can be surrounded with so much warmth that it comes forth of its own accord. Once when I was in the Middle East a tour guide kept pointing out how the sheep of the area knew to follow their shepherd. They knew the sound of his voice. We frequently saw sheep single file following their shepherd across the fields. Then when passing through a small town soon afterward, we were delayed by a shepherd who was standing in the middle of the road obviously driving his sheep. When I asked why these sheep did not obey their shepherd as the others did, the guide replied: "That's not the shepherd; that's the butcher." Too many evangelistic approaches smack of hammers and butchers. Warmth and gentleness, love and patience work far better. Let me illustrate.

Recently I was flying between Tulsa and Detroit. It was the end of a semester and I had some papers that I desperately needed to grade. As I approached my seat, I realized that an attractive woman was sitting in the seat next to mine. I thought to myself that if I could just get my briefcase out and get my papers on my lap before she spoke, I was safe. I would not have to engage her in conversation. Well into my second paper she suddenly looked at me and said, "You are grading papers. What do you teach?" I replied, "Theology." She then asked, "Where do you teach?" I replied "Oral Roberts University." She responded, "Oh, really, I've never heard of that; where is it located? I replied, "Have you ever heard of Oral Roberts?" She answered, "No."

At that point I simply folded my papers, put the away, and did what I should have done to begin with—address her fairly and openly. I turned to her saying: "Tell me about yourself." She began to tell me how wonderful her life was. Then, without my being aware of the transition, she began to describe just how miserable she was. She started asking me questions. At one point she remarked, "I know that these are stupid questions." I replied quite sincerely, "Lady, I've never heard such intelligent questions in all my life. Please ask on." Would you like to know what her last questions was? "Bob, what's to prevent me from putting my faith and trust in Jesus Christ right now?" It took me hours to come to earth even after the plane had landed.

Opportunities for evangelism are all around us. People are vulnerable to a listening ear. They are not accustomed to being listened to as if they had something important to say. The lady on the plane set the agenda. All I did was listen and answer her questions. She, in effect, led herself to Christ. God is at work. He wants to bless. Furthermore, He wants to use us as an intrument of that blessing. He wants to bless others. And, if we take Him seriously, He might well bless us in the blessing.

Let me tell you another story that makes a similar point. A friend of mine (we will call him George) was just leaving his office in a large midwestern church. As he opened the door to leave, someone else was opening the door to enter. The two of them stood there for a moment, practically nose-to-nose. The one entering looked to be a beggar. He had not shaved in some weeks. His clothes were tattered. His breath reeked of alcohol. Without waiting for an introduction, he quickly asked my friend if he could spare a few dollars for something to eat. He stated that he had no money and that he had not eaten for several days. George's first thought was to give him the money, but then on instinct, said "No." The other man recoiled, "You mean you, one of the ministers in this big church, can't spare a few bucks for someone less fortunate?" Again, George replied, "No!" Again, the other said, "Can you lend me just two dollars for a sandwich and a bowl of soup?" George smiled and said, "No, but I am going to lunch, I'll take you with me." Somewhat taken aback, the other, before he could react, found himself joining George for lunch at the restaurant nearby.

As the two men waited for their orders, George asked the

man, "What's your name?" Immediately the man slammed his fist on the table and replied, "That's just the problem with you preachers! You don't care about me! You just want to know my name." George, somewhat startled, answered, "Listen, friend, you haven't shaved for weeks. Your clothes are tattered, and you stink to high heaven. But, who knows, some day down the road you just might decide to clean up your act, and I won't even recognize you. The only common denominator might well be your name." The meal passed in silence. As they rose to leave, George asked if he could take the man somewhere, to which the man replied, "I wouldn't ride across the street with you." George went one way the man the other.

As George was conducting a wedding ceremony that evening, he looked up through the dimly lit church building and noticed a man sitting high in the balcony. It looked like his ill-mannered lunch companion. After the service, he went to the balcony, saw that it was indeed the man, and sat down beside him. It was about 8:00 P.M. Five hours later, both men were still sitting there but neither had uttered the first word. At that time, George assured the man that he was welcome to remain in the building, but that he needed some sleep as he had to preach the next morning. Again, on impulse, he turned to the man and asked, "If you could preach to these people tomorrow morning, what would you say to them?" The man replied instantly, "Don't give a man 2 bucks; take him to lunch." Then, as if the pump had been primed, the story came rolling out. Five years earlier, the man had prepared the best sermon of his career. He went to church to preach it, but went right on going. He had been "going" ever since. George suggested that they might call the man's home to see if anyone was still there. The man stated that he had been out of touch for so long that he did not know if they were even still in the same town. George said, "Let's call collect, Then, at least, we'll know the lay of the land." They called. The man's wife answered. She had been waiting patiently and, believe it or not, asked the man, no, begged the man to come home. He agreed. George first offered to take him to the airport, but the man preferred the bus, as he needed a little additional time to make the necessary adjustment. At the bus station, George pulled out his wallet to pay for the man's ticket, but the man pushed it away saying that he did not need it. He then pulled out a wad of bills, including several thousand dollar bills and many more hundreds, fifties, twenties, and tens. George, totally shocked, asked the man, "Where in the world did you get that?" The man's reply were the last words he uttered as he entered the bus, "From do-gooders, social workers, and preachers just like you."

The moral of that story is fairly straightforward. Lord, give us caring hearts, patient minds, and wisdom to speak when the time is right. I sometimes feel that given five hours with anyone is license to tell him or her everything I know. The truth of the matter is that if they do not know I love them and care for them, I had better walk softly in their life or they will have me for breakfast. On the other hand, given enough time, needs surface within a loving, caring relationship to which the gospel can be applied.

ESTABLISHING A LOVING, CARING RELATIONSHIP

Again, people are vulnerable. A single word from just the right person can put almost anyone on top or underneath. Small wonder God calls us to be first of all a lover of people. Several months ago I decided to do a study on some of the common denominators present in the ministry of Jesus. What was the character of His anointing? Sometimes when attempting to evangelize, I am keenly aware that I am on my own. I sense no power to witness. I seem to be ministering out of my own strength. At other times, however, I am almost overwhelmed with an awareness of God's grace at work in a given situation. My question? How can I be more consistent, more like Jesus?

As I searched the Scriptures, I soon discovered that when Jesus' ministry was most evident, almost inevitably I would turn the page and find one word—compassion. "And he had compassion upon them" (e.g., Matt. 9:36; 14:14; 15:32; Luke 7:13; 10:33). I will long remember the words of George Whitefield who stated that when he stood to preach before the people, he saw two things—their hurt and their mortality. Clearly, once the gospel core is understood and our sphere is established, we must then seek to secure the kind of loving, caring relationship out of which needs can surface.

Recently, I came to realize that there is gifted preaching, but there are also great preachers. Gifted preaching has the ability to excite the masses, whereas great preachers have the ability to stir the soul. The same is true for evangelism. Some evangelism excites the masses, but some evangelists stir the soul. The object is not to tickle the fancy, but to scratch the itch. Evangelism is deep when it makes us deep. Unassimilated evangelism is obscure and makes us obscure. Our objective is not simply to attract an interest in our understanding, but to move people to an understanding themselves. All too often I find that I spend too much time being angry at sin, and not enough time loving the sinner. Frequently I find myself asking God to sweeten me up.

Much of relational evangelism is built on a person's ability to empathize, to see the world as God sees it. I am much easier to take if you can see me as you see your own children. I find that I am so much more effective if I can see as God sees, love as God loves, care as God cares. Now do not misunderstand me; although His Spirit does dwell within me I am not God. Nonetheless, as Christians we sense God's love stirring within us. In fact, Jesus Himself sets the precedent for this kind of ministry. *The great commandment governs the great commission.* We are not ready to go into all the world until we first love our neighbor as ourselves. Compassion always precedes program.

Jesus stirred the crowds, but realized the crowds once persuaded for, can be twice persuaded against. His long-term legacy was a Spirit-filled loving and caring building of relationships. He amazed the multitudes, but He healed the leper. Most people are won to Christ out of a one-on-one relationship. Ministry almost always knows my name. I am rarely a nameless face among nameless faces.

Emily, in Thornton Wilder's *Our Town,* stands alone on that empty stage at the end of a disappointing day crying, "Won't somebody out there look at me?" I once attended an international conference of evangelists. I was convinced that I was the only noncelebrity out of 4,000 participants. Time and again I would engage one of these celebrities, only to be dismissed after thirty seconds with the apology, "Oh, excuse me, Dr. Tuttle (as the person stooped to read my name off my tag), I must see that person over there. I've been looking for him for three days." After nearly a week of this, I remember engaging another whom I had admired and respected for years. He actually sat there and looked at me for several hours, apparently interested in what I had to say. I have never forgotten him. I have probably recommended more of his books than any other. Does that astonish you?

People need to be loved. Genuine love is almost irresistible. If we take time to establish a caring relationship, the needs (almost as if they had been waiting to surface) reveal themselves in amazing ways.

MEETING THE NEED

Once the relationship has been established and the need has surfaced, then we need to accept our responsibility for ministry. Admittedly, I do not have all the answers. Again, truth remains truth, regardless of what I think about it. Yet, evangelism at some point has to be intentional. I believe (right or wrong) that I have the answer. His name is Jesus. So, I want to be humble, but not too humble. As Christians, we believe that God has done something for us, and that He will do something for others. God never promises that we will not experience trouble, but He does promise that we need never be defeated. Interestingly enough, the answer itself is not an idea, a philosophy, or a formula; *it is a relationship*. It is a relationship with a living God. Again, relational evangelism does not mean that we need not be intentional. We stated earlier that in order to evangelize effectively, we establish a relationship. But then, we offer Jesus. Anything less than Jesus as the answer is a rope of sand. More will be said in the next chapter about the answer we offer.

APOSTOLIC EYES

In conclusion, let us review one important aspect common to the chapter as a whole. Christians see people as God sees them. Christians do not see as the world sees. The world frequently sees people as scenery or machinery. The Christian sees people as potential followers of Jesus Christ—a part of His living body. The world talks and reacts. The Christian listens, reflects, and then responds. The world looks to its own needs. The Christian steps out in ministry, trusting God to supply the gifts necessary to meet the needs of others. "God, give us apostolic eyes. Let us see the needs of the world. Let us meet those needs by Your grace." After all, that is precisely what evangelism is all about.

Chapter 11
Applying God's Answer, Keep It Simple

Evangelism is divine reality, channeled through human potential, directed toward a people in need.

If we have done our homework and have built a proper relationship, the transition between people's needs and God's answer is easily accomplished. Once people realize that the house is on fire, they can quickly be moved to action. The problem, however, is that it is frequently difficult to convince people of any imminent danger. Much of our culture has lost its sensitivity to heat and smoke. Guilt is out; doubt is in.

We have sought to establish the fact that a solid relationship resensitizes us to need. Although people tend to cover up their needs in the face of superficiality they will surface within an atmosphere of love and acceptance. Then, as the needs surface within a relationship, we can apply the gospel naturally, yet with significant impact.

As people "out there" are unaware that their felt needs are spiritual, they are also unaware that the answer is *ultimately* spiritual. Much of the world sees its problems in simpler terms such as, I need this, or I need that. I hurt here, or I hurt there. Actually, most problems are more complex, but the answer can be simple. Note that I do not say simplistic. The simplistic answer fails to take the problem seriously. It lacks empathy. It often neglects any immediate or physical need (food for the hungry or clothes for the naked). The simple gospel meets any immediate need and then makes the spiritual solution clearly understood. Again, once a spiritual need arises (especially within a solid relationship), the good news of Jesus Christ can be applied with care and understanding. So why make it so complicated?

AGAINST SUBLIME DIVINITY

John Wesley once wrote, "My soul is sick of the sublime divinity. Let *me* think and speak as a little child! Let *my* religion be plain, artless, simple."[1] As complicated as the application (that is, getting someone to respond) might seem, God's answer is not a riddle cloaked in an enigma, wrapped in mystery. It can be made simple enough to be understood by all. That, by the way, is our task. *We* cannot change anyone, but we can make the answer simple enough so that the Holy Spirit can begin (or continue) *His* work.

Recently I heard a message by Gordon Hunter on the simplicity of the gospel that moved me greatly. Some of the following illustrations were given in that message as a part of the contrast. Here is a definition of religious experience, for example: "The more courageously truth is objectively sought and understanding taught by the honest religionist, the more probability will be that he will engage intuitive inspiration towards experiencing extension of participating environmental oneness in supreme cosmic being and divine inanimate/animate spiritual concerns through successive evolutions towards evermore enticingly advancing goals." Hunter calls that "galloping gobbledygook." Why not make it simple? Romans 10:9 is simple enough. John 1:12 is also to the point. Why not "believe on the Lord Jesus Christ and you shall be saved"? Really, doesn't that say it better?

Let me share with you only one section of a rewrite of the Lord's Prayer. It goes something like this, "We respectively petition, request, and entreat that an adequate provision be made this day and the date herein after subscribed, for the organizing of such methods of allocations and distribution as may be deemed necessary and proper to assure the reception by and for said petitioners of such quantities of baked cereal products as shall, in the judgment of the aforesaid petitioners, constitute a sufficient supply thereof." Jesus made it simple, "Give us this day our daily bread."

Recently this statement appeared in a Christian education magazine advertising material for church school teachers, "Action-oriented orchestration of innovative inputs, generated by the escalation of meaningful indigenous decision-making dialogue, can maximize the vital thrust towards non-alienated and viable introstructure." Yet many churches buy material advertised in such a matter. Little wonder that I rarely ask a theologian a question and I understand the answer. Yet, the problem is hardly confinded to theologians. In Texas the following explanation describes something familiar to us all: "Terminal behavior objectives for continuous progression modules in early childhood education" describes—what else?—a report card. Little wonder a 32-page booklet was drafted to explain it and then a pamphlet was prepared to explain the booklet. It reminds me of a rewrite of an old nursery rhyme. "Mary had a little lamb, its fleece electrostatic, and everywhere that Mary went, the lights became erratic. It followed her to school one day, electrodes all a-jingle; it made the children's hair stand up; it made their fingers tingle. The teacher tried to put it out; her body it was grounded. The flash was seen for miles around; she has not yet rebounded."

As is often the case, Charlie Brown makes the point. In a cartoon strip, we see him knocking on Lucy's door and asking her if she would like for him to shovel the snow from her walk. Lucy replies, "Yes, but first sign this contract: 'You will work for a flat fee, provide your own lunch, and pay your own insurance. If it snows again within 24 hours, the sidewalk must be cleaned again without charge. We also have exclusive rights to your shovel. We reserve all T.V., motion picture, radio, and video cassette rights in perpetuity. If you whistle while you work, all recording becomes our property. The area to be shoveled runs from the porch to the street.' Here, sign the bottom line." Charlie's reply, "The contract is longer than the sidewalk." Little wonder Einstein wanted only one tie. More than one made life too complicated. Please keep it simple. Jesus sets the precedent.

The average reader can read (slowly) all of the words of Jesus in less than two hours. His parables are so profound that theologians cannot exhaust them; but are so simple that a child in church school can understand them. The great words of the gospel are plain and simple words—man, life, love, child, home, pain, hope. . . . Jesus spoke of a farmer plowing a field, a woman cooking a meal, a carpenter building a house, a shepherd minding his sheep, fishermen going over their catch, children playing, grapes growing, a rich man inviting friends to a banquet. Even those things beyond mere words He describes in term of two of the most common things around—bread and wine. The Beatitudes contain 117 words; 95 have but one syllable. The Lord's Prayer has 66 words; 46 have one syllable, 14 have two syllables, and only four as many as three syllables. God wants to reveal Himself, to make Himself known. He is not out to catch anyone on the fine print. He is not the divine concealer. He is the divine revealer. Keep it simple.

Elton Trueblood states that the mark of maturity is to believe fewer doctrines with greater intensity. Although we might not agree, all of us know what he means. The object of good biblical interpretation is to simplify. Those who study the Bible as a part of their academic training know that we can identify later manuscripts by virtue of their greater simplicity. It has always been out task to make it relevant and understood. This brings us back to the answer itself.

JESUS IS LORD, TRUE SIMPLICITY

In Part I, we sought to establish that the phrase, "Jesus is Lord," is the shortest, earliest, and greatest of the Christian creeds. Again, this is not simplistic. Its true simplicity comes only after one understands its profound complexity. Its profundity touches the very depths of life, but it is utterly simple in its essence.

Jesus is Lord. This, for me, has become the *whole* of life. Last year my home was robbed. I remember the sick feeling that someone had violated the place where I live. Then it hit me. Not one of those things stolen owned any part of me, and when they were taken, those who took them, took none of me with them. That is freedom, the kind of freedom people want to experience. You can take away all that I have, and I will survive. Take away my faith in Jesus Christ, and I am a dead man. It is just that simple.

Thoreau said that life moves toward perfection, not when there is nothing more to be gained, but when there is nothing more to be taken away. "Having nothing, we have everything" within the context of the gospel is simplicity indeed. Mother Teresa went to Calcutta with nothing but a rosary and two dollars. Wesley owned two silver spoons and a few books; Gandhi, a loin cloth. Perhaps those who insist that all we really need is a New Testament and a pail are right.

Please make it simple. I am told that all major breakthroughs in science turn out to be a reduction from complexity to simplicity. Scientific discovery does not invent truth; it uncovers, or at best, confirms it. The cure for cancer is probably under our noses. It is interesting how the electronics industry has simplified the test tube to the transistor and then simplified the transistor to the printed circuit. The nations of the world ponder the solution to inflation. After all is said and done, the problem increases until we find a way to overcome one thing—*greed*. Capitalism, for example, works only when free enterprise produces better products and services, not avarice and greed. We live in a "uni-verse" There is *one* truth and truth is *one*. Little wonder Paul expresses the fear that the Corinthians might lose their single-hearted devotion (2 Cor. 11:1–6).

Life is an entrance and an exit, with a little in between. If we come *for* nothing, we go *to* nothing, then there is nothing in between. Life has meaning because we were born for a purpose. That purpose is fulfilled through faith in Jesus Christ. Our identity is in Him. We do not know who we are until we know Him. Jesus is Lord means that life in Him is what gets us out of bed seven mornings a week. Again, my identity is in Him. The question, "Who am I" alludes not just to my name, my job, or where I live. I am *me* because my spirit dwells within me. We are the body of Jesus Christ because His Spirit dwells within us. He truly is the friend who sticks closer than a brother. Listen how Peter identifies himself, "[I am] an apostle of Jesus Christ" (1 Peter 1:1). An effective evangelistic tool could be the simple telling a friend who you are without mentioning your name, your job, or where you live. Think about it.

Oh, Lord, keep me simple and simply Thine!

DO NOT ARGUE

I have a haunting feeling that Jesus walks out when the argument begins. I frequently win theological debates, but I have yet to win anyone to Jesus Christ through such debates. The reason for this is, again, at the heart of our faith. Religious argument is a poor tool for evangelism. It invites resistance. In fact, good theology itself is not a very effective evangelistic tool. God uses some of the strangest things to get people converted. Although good theology will deliver you from a multitude of bondage, people are rarely converted through the turn of a clever phrase or a sound theological deposition.

Religion is people searching for God. Christianity is God searching for people. Of course, there is a religious aspect to Christianity; but that is the *form* not the *power* of the gospel. The power of the gospel is the grace of God released through faith in Jesus Christ. This would suggest basically two schools of thought. Let me describe them to you briefly in an attempt to demonstrate the futility of argument where evangelism is concerned.

There is a fundamental difference between the Roman Catholic and the Protestant position as to how one experiences God, or perhaps more accurately, how one comes to a knowledge of God. This is not to say who is right and who is wrong; it is simply to say that they disagree. They may both be wrong, but they cannot both be right. Let me explain.

Catholic theology builds out of a Thomistic mold. Thomism is the name given to a school of philosophy that follows the tenets elaborated by Thomas Aquinas (c. 1225–1274). In a phrase, *reason leads to faith* (or grace). As a result of the Fall, man is corrupted only from the "neck down." The mind or the intellect is left free to reason with the heart; in effect, maneuvering it into a position of faith. You might state the case in this way: beginning with sensible things (nature) our intellect is led to the point of knowing about God (grace), that He exists (the cosmological argument). To state the same case a bit differently, Aquinas insisted that knowledge originates in sensations of a physical world that man's reason is equipped to know. Natural reason is adequate for a knowledge of God's existence, but this knowledge is *completed* and *perfected* by the Christian revelation. Since Pius X (1835–1914, the Pope from 1903), this has been *the* Catholic philosophy. Now the point I am making here is not that this is wrong, but that this is fundamentally different from the Protestant position. Again, let me explain.

Protestants generally agree that *all* true knowledge of God *begins* (is not only completed and perfected) with faith. Following the "Augustinian-Francescan School of Fideists" (to which Aquinas was reacting), Protestants insist that "one believes in order to understand." In other words, one is totally corrupt (including the mind), without the true knowledge of God, until the Spirit of God enlightens us by faith. Again, in a phrase, *faith leads to reason* (or understanding). Now please do not think that I am splitting theological hairs. Coleridge said it well, "One can either be a Platonist or an

Aristotelian, but one cannot be both simultaneously." Either one reasons one's way inductively to a knowledge of God, or one's faith in God, as a point of departure, enables one to understand *deductively* a knowledge of God.

Argument fails in evangelism at the point of its attempt to enter through the human in order to reach the divine. Protestant theology objects to this along the lines of 1 Corinthians 2:6–16 (especially vv. 12 and 14). In those verses the point is that the unspiritual man or woman is not able to understand the things of God because they are spiritually discerned. Please take time to compare Ephesians 3:1–13 (the human mind cannot fathom the mystery of God). Compare also 2 Corinthians 11:3 (we should not be led astray from our simplicity). To put all of this still another way, Roman Catholics believe that God helps those who help themselves. Protestants, by and large, believe that God helps those who cannot help themselves.

All of this points to the mystery of God. I have always had a great deal of respect for the references to "mystery" in Ephesians 3. We mentioned earlier that much of our western culture has been left-brain oriented (the cognitive and rational). Jesus is Lord refers to a right-brain (the intuitive, spiritual, mystical) function. The left side of the brain argues with God as if to make Him prove Himself. The right side of the brain takes God at His word and receives His gift as a little child. Remember, a child-like faith is not childishness. A child-like faith is satisfied with a reasonable response to difficult questions. The skeptic is not satisfied with any response, no matter how reasonable.

Make it simple. Whatever it takes to communicate Jesus is Lord is the heart of our gospel communication. Do not argue. Share who you are, not merely your name, your job, or where you live. Relational evangelism makes the application of the gospel or the transition between the need and God's answer natural. Let me illustrate. I am told that it is difficult to understand love and forgiveness on the vertical plane (that is between oneself and God), until we have first of all been loved and forgiven on the horizontal plane. If that is true, and I suspect it is, then someone "out there" is waiting to be loved and forgiven by you or he or she will have a difficult time understanding God's love and forgiveness. What about your neighbor, that person down the street or at work? Have you considered offering forgiveness to someone out there that he or she might understand forgiveness from on high? If Jesus is Lord, then He moves us toward those in need. If the action is motivated by love, then the grace of God is already at work, eager to change, willing to empower, waiting for faith. The simple gospel is that God is after the one who is lost. As evangelists, each day we pray that the Holy Spirit will plumb some new depth of our experience. In our own silence, we ask that same Spirit to reveal some area of resistance. As we yield that area of resistance to God, the Holy Spirit moves to that low pressure, changing us from within and motivating us toward a people in need.

---

[1]John Wesley, *Works*, 3rd Ed. (Zondervan Reprint n.d.) Vol. 1, p. 256.

Chapter 12
A Case Study

This case attempts to demonstrate the potential effectiveness of a solid relationship for allowing needs to surface and then applying God's answer.

THE CASE: "ANOTHER DAY OLDER AND DEEPER IN DEBT"

For the first time in his life, Bill Rhodes was looking forward to work. The job was the same, but he was different. For more than twenty years he had been a first-class assemblyman in the Ford plant in Dearborn, Michigan. For the past ten years he had worked at the same spot on the line. Although he had never complained, he had been secretly afraid that he was becoming the part that he was installing. Now that fear was gone. Today would be different, a new beginning. As he dressed for work, he recalled his promise to God made a few moments earlier. "God, if You will make me aware of the need, even if it is Big John, I'll try to meet that need and speak a word for You. You open the door and I'll walk through it." Bill then thought to himself, I'm important. Someone needs me. I'm not just another day older and deeper in debt. As Bill stepped out the door, he chuckled to himself. "Hello, world, here comes Bill Rhodes; I'm a child of the King. Someone out there needs me. Who is it, Lord? Is it Big John? Perhaps it is Betty or Benny or Natkowski. I don't care. I love them all!"

Background

Bill's normal rountine is to get up at 4:45 A.M. He eats breakfast at the cafe just down the street. Betty is usually his waitress. It is the end of her shift. Over the months she has come to trust Bill. Although she is normally cheerful to the other customers, she frequently complains to Bill. Her life is hectic. She must be home before the kids (a girl 6 and a boy 14) are off to school. The girl is sheer joy, while the boy is starting to be a problem. She suspects that he is experimenting with drugs and sex. There is no real hassle, just constant pressure. Bill is always sympathetic. He listens, but rarely says anything other than that she might try seeing a social worker.

Bill gets to work early in order to get the freshest sandwiches from the catering truck parked in the lot outside the plant. Henry, the owner of the truck, is a friend of some ten years. He, too, trusts Bill. Henry frequently describes his dream for retirement, a cabin in the Upper Peninsula. Bill listens sympathetically but says little.

Big John (who stands 5′ 6″) works next to him on the line. He is a bit of a sorehead. He is always complaining. He seems perpetually bored. He makes a game (although he would lose his job the moment he was caught) of slipping various parts into his lunchbox. Bill usually avoids him at break time, as do most of the other workers.

Bennett (called Benny; Bill never knew his first name) is the clown. He is always joking, though rarely at someone else's expense. Benny never reveals himself. Bill knows almost nothing about him; but he is good company so he usually takes his breaks with him. Bill laughts at his jokes, although most are a bit crude and off-color.

Bill's immediate boss is an ex-Air Force master sergeant who prides himself on running a tight ship. He retired at forty-one and now works the floor as superintendent (he considers himself lucky for getting first-shift work and, after all, this is just as challenging as his work in the Force. Although he wanted a position in aircraft maintenance, he had been "stuck" in the motor pool, servicing staff cars). He also had enough versatility to fill in at most points along the line when the workmen failed to show up or called in sick. His name is Natkowski. He is a Catholic who takes his religion seriously, though he rarely talks about it.

Bill's job is monotonous. His responsibility is to set the steering column at the "drop," an important job as jobs here go. This is the spot where the parts become an automobile. The body, which has been assembled along one line, is here lowered onto the chassis, which has been assembled along another. It is at this point that the plant accountant (so Bill is frequently reminded) computes their loss or gain. If the plant could just keep up the volume, the gain or profit would be phenomenal. Exactly how much it actually costs to make an automobile is as closely guarded a secret as Colonel Sanders' herbs-and-spices recipe for Kentucky Fried Chicken. Bill tries not to think about this. After all, jobs are scarce in the industry and he is paid fairly well. For years that is all that really mattered.

Johnny

On his way home from work, Bill has been stopping off for a paper at the newsstand a block from his house. He could have had it delivered, but he uses the excuse of the late edition in order to chat briefly with Johnny, whose father owns the stand, although Johnny works it after school. Johnny is just seventeen. Bill has noticed something different about him. He really seems to care! Oh, he is like most kids in a lot of ways. He is crazy about sports. He follows almost everything from boxing to golf. He talks like a veteran announcer when discussing the Lions or the Pistons, whom they both follow religiously.

At the beginning of the summer Johnny had had an accident. He had lost the use of an arm while snatching a small child from the path of a van whose fender caught it just above the elbow as he whirled around to run. He had made the front page of the local section of the paper he sold. Bill, quite frankly, was curious. Johnny spoke about life as if were an opportunity—a gift. It wasn't just his idealistic youth either. He really looked forward to life, although the accident had eliminated any prospect of a sporting career.

A few months earlier, Bill was heading home from work and his mind was on the errand his wife, Clara, had given him that morning. He was to buy a special kind of bread at the market, but he could not remember the name. He had lost the note she had given him and he was rummaging through his pockets, cursing to himself as he approached

Johnny's newsstand. Johnny sensed his frustration and carefully asked what the problem was. Could he help? Bill was amazed that he should even notice. Johnny seemed interested. Bill wondered why he should care. He had problems of his own. Johnny insisted on asking a friend in the shop behind the stand, since she was sure to know. Johnny's face beamed as he came out of the shop, not with the name, but the loaf of bread itself. Bill was grateful, though a little embarrassed, and Johnny never mentioned it again. Bill, however, thought about it for at least a week. He found himself trusting Johnny, just as his waitress friend, Betty, trusted him. There seemed to be little threat. If he did not like the occasional words of advice (though he usually listened), he could disregard it because, after all, Johnny was only a kid, and what did he know? Johnny was either extremely bright or something worse. Bill found himself captured. Johnny hinted that there was something more to life that could bring hope, if not excitement, to what was normally dull and routine.

Bill found himself thinking more and more, not only about Johnny, but about what he said. He actually could not wait to see him and was greatly disappointed when Johnny was forced to take a few days off for physical therapy in a Detroit hospital. Then, just a month ago, Johnny had dropped by Bill's house to borrow some pliers to cut baling wire. His had been ripped off. Bill was more than willing to lend the tool, as he was anxious to be relieved of some of the debt of Johnny's favor. He was, however, puzzled as he remembered Johnny saying happily, "Praise God for friends who care enough to trust a friend. Thanks, Bill, for being my friend." The next day, the pliers were returned with a note saying, "Thanks for being a friend."

A few days later, Bill and Johnny were watching the first preseason Lions game together. Johnny shared more and more about the life that really mattered. Eventually, Bill began asking questions. He even accepted an invitation for him and Clara to attend an evening fellowship group. As a part of that group, both Bill and Clara were soon soundly converted. Bill was so turned on that he went directly to Betty, Henry, Benny, Natkowski, and even Big John, but at every turn, the door was slammed shut.

The Lesson Learned

Since his conversion, Bill had begun to understnad why those doors had been shut. Whereas previously he had been the listener; now, he had the answers.This was an adjustment for both Bill and his friends. Since he had been renewed, the relationships had to be renewed. He was truly different. For several months he had sought to reestablish contact with all of his friends, although he was extremely low key with regard to his religious experience. Interestingly enough, his friends were beginning to open up. A few were even starting to ask questions. In the meantime, Bill was busily learning the basic content of the gospel. He was also realizing that his ministry, by and large, would surface within his normal routine. Bill welcomed this. He wanted his normal routine to count for something with God, lest his normal routine remain just that—normal routine—with no other purpose than a paycheck at the end of the week.

The previous week, Bill had begun moving toward Big John, who at first was suspicious, but was now beginning to warm up. They had lunch together on two occasions. Big John, too, was beginning to ask questions. Again, Bill thought to himself that if Big John would respond to his presentation of the gospel, then the other possibilities were endless.

The night before, Bill and Clara had attended another fellowship group. Bill felt that the discussion was aimed at him. They had studied Joshua 3, and Bill had been especially moved by the prophetic utterances. In them were both warning and promise. If the warning was his, then so was the promise! Bill decided to claim Joshua 3:5, "Consecrate yourselves, for tomorrow the LORD will do amazing things among you."

This was the day. Bill did not know what to expect. The beginning might be small. As he walked toward the cafe, he again said to himself, "Someone out there needs me." Then, once again, he prayed to God, "Who is it, Lord? I don't care. I love them all!"

DISCUSSION GUIDE

This case is an attempt to demonstrate both the potential and the problems for ministry within the normal routine. Sometimes we do not realize that when we are converted, we need to reestablish relationships on the basis of our new identity. Bill failed to do that at first and the doors were shut, but now that he has taken time to prepare in his own understanding of the gospel and to reestablish a solid relationship as a follower of Jesus Christ, his anticipation is high.

Questions to Consider:

1. Bill's immediate expectations are built on a scriptural prophecy. Is this wise?
2. What could Bill learn from his conversion? What does Johnny teach us about the value of building relationships into an opportunity for evangelism?
3. Discuss some of the possibilities with regard to the various characters mentioned in the case. When needs become known, we need to be able to recognize them. Are there any clues as to some specific needs that might begin to reveal themselves?
4. Where does Clara fit in? What might her role be? She has very little contact with Bill's sphere of influence, but how might she be involved in his ministry, as well as her own?
5. How might you describe "God's answer" to some of Bill's friends?

Part IV

Follow-up, the Indispensable Task

Chapter 13
Follow-up Through Continuing Relationships

Evangelism is the "go" of the great commission ruled by the "love" of the great commandment.

I am increasingly concerned with Christians who have apparently lost their "first love." If their salvation is maintained, their Christian walk certainly is not. They return as a dog to its vomit. As Christians we are rightfully concerned for our unsaved loved ones. Jim Buskirk, Dean of the School of Theology at Oral Roberts University, insists that we should be equally concerned for our unloved saved ones. My father, Robert Tuttle, Sr., recently published a book entitled *Born Again: What Then*? He raises the question: "Once converted, how do we as Christians develop a style of spirituality that will make us vibrant and healthy?" The answer? In part, we keep on growing. Growth is absolutely essential for life as a Christian.

In the introduction we stated that John Wesley insisted that to lead people to Jesus Christ without also providing an adequate opportunity for growth and nurture is simply, "to beget children for the murderer." In fact, he became so frustrated with backsliding that at one point he admitted that he would far rather *retain* than *gain*. Part IV of this book has to do with retaining once the decision to follow Christ has been made. That means that we keep Christians growing. I am personally convinced that the only way to keep Christians alive is to keep them moving. The Christian walk is much like riding a bicycle; we are either moving forward or falling off. Thus, the heading for this part is: "Follow-up, the Indispensable Task."

In Part III we stated that the contact between a needy people and God's answer is crucial. We also stated that relational evangelism enables a person to make the necessary transition without embarrassment and within a context of genuine interest and concern. Relational evangelism has another equally important function, however. It is most effective in terms of follow-up. Since out witness is usually to those with whom we come into contact daily, maintaining that contact is vitually assured. That is as it should be. Again, follow-up is essential. Follow-up, however, is multifaceted. It includes both direction and fellowship as key ingredients. In this chapter we will look at the continuing relationship in terms of discipleship. In the next chapter we will speak about overcoming sin—sanctification within the context of a dynamic community. The chapter following that will consider the role of the Holy Spirit in all of this.

THE PROCESS OF DISCIPLING

Discipling is a process of involving new Christians in the kind of relationship in which there is specific instruction as to how to live out one's walk in the Spirit. Corrie Ten Boom has entitled a book, *Not Good If Detached.* Taking those words from a book of train tickets, she applied them to the Christian walk. Her point is well made. Another book by Reuben Welsh, *We Really Do Need Each Other,* makes a similar point. As Christians, we must always be in relationship to one another. To risk making an absolute statement, there really is no other way to live victoriously.

Although we can in most cases maintain some contact, it may not be possible to meet weekly with all those we seek to evangelize. A significant number, however, would be more than willing to ensure survival by attaching themselves to one who would monitor their growth and development. Christian pediatrics is becoming more and more of a science. Over the past ten years, several good books have been written about discipling baby Christians. One of the best is by Robert Coleman—*The Master Plan of Evangelism.* In that book, he depicts Jesus spending most of His time with only twelve disciples. Jesus was selective. He was also a master at "show and tell." He was constantly demonstrating His method. For example, He prayed so well that His disciples asked Him to teach them to pray like that. He ministered so effectively that His disciples asked Him to teach them to minister like that. Coleman points out that Jesus picked a few, taught them by example, and prepared them to reproduce on their own. Through discipling, evangelism is more than growth by addition; it is growth by multiplication. We not only lead people to Christ, we train them to lead (and then train) others to Christ as well. Let me mention only three general rules in this process.

First, choose only a few. If we cannot minister effectively to everyone, then our sphere of influence is even smaller with regard to those we might wish to disciple. In every place I have lived since becoming a Christian, I have always found a few who would commit themselves to spend time with me every week. One such person was a kid off the street. Another was a recently converted atheist. Still another was a man in prison. Another was a man with a "terminal" illness. As mentioned earlier, since I have been teaching in a theological seminary, I have met personally with a few students each week for the purpose of discipling. Let me suggest a few guidelines for selecting the kind of person I think would be good for discipleship where evangelism is concerned.

Find some within your sphere of influence who want to bear witness to what God is doing in their lives. They do not have to be articulate, as such, simply willing. Let me give you an example.

Douglas Hyde's book, *Dedication and Leadership*, speaks of a man named Jim. Hyde, an ex-Communist turned Christian, was conducting a leadership course for a group of party members while still a Communist in a London borough. He was addressing a number of interested party prospects and had just stated that the Communists would take anyone who was willing to be trained in leadership and turn him or her into a leader. As life would have it, a man stepped forward. Hyde describes him as "very short, grotesquely fat, with a flabby white face, a cast in one eye, and to make matters worse, a more distressing stutter." Jim was an electrician. After some months of careful indoctrination, Jim was sent to teach a beginners course to ordinary building workers like himself, drawn from the same building site. In spite of the obvious drawbacks, Jim's life changed. In fact, his speech impediment frequently worked in his favor as he evoked sympathy from the crowd. In short, Jim became a productive Communist. Hyde's point? If the Communist promoting an ideal can do it; Christians can do it promoting the God/man Jesus Christ.

Other guidelines might include teachableness. I always respond to someone who is open and eager to learn. I never expect persons to believe everything I tell them, although I do expect them to believe that I believe everything I tell them. It is not important for them to swallow whole a particular point of view, but it is important for them to try to understand what I am attempting to teach them without automatic resistance to every new idea.

Find those with big hearts. Compassion is almost always a key. When Christ comes into our lives, He enables us to see the world as God sees it. Persons who want to gather the world into their arms and love it into submission are always good prospects for discipleship.

Finally, find those who "hunger and thirst for righteousness." Again, I respond to those who yearn for God. That is almost always a good ingredient for discipleship.

A second general rule in the discipleship process is that we are to model it. This is a most important concept. We must be willing to "flesh" it out. A solid relationship communicates at a level far deeper than words alone. We not only speak our faith; we live it out. We live it out in the "trenches" where people are trying to cope, trying to survive. Too many of us have little or no awareness of persons "out there" needing us in a vital relationship. Consequently, we are unaware of being watched. If we are living victorious lives, we can well believe that the world is watching. Many people out there are bored with the routine of getting up, going to work, coming home, watching T.V., and going to bed. They want something more. As Christians, we can provide an alternative. Whether we are aware of it or not, we are modeling our faith.

Recently my secretary interrupted a class that I was teaching to hand me a note. The interruption annoyed me. I said nothing to her, accepted the note, placed it on the desk in front of me, and continued my lecture. She then excused herself somewhat apologetically. As I continued the lecture, my students seemed restless. I could no longer engage them. Then it hit me! Without my saying a word, my secretary had sensed my irritation. Even more to the point, the students had sensed my shortness with my secretary. I was being watched. I was teaching one thing, but modeling another. My reaction? I dismissed the class long enough to seek out my secretary and apologize. Then, and only then, could the lecture continue. Again, whether we are aware of it or not, we are modeling our faith. So, why not be intentional—a little of the "show and tell" ourselves? Even if our gift is not to lead someone to Christ, per se, we can attach ourselves to a few struggling Christians and demonstrate the path along which we can all move toward greater maturity. Again, model it. "Do as I say, not as I do" will not cut it. Either we live it or bury it. In a discipling relationship, we can be "smoked out" too easily if we are not congruent with what we say and do. Time and again, Jesus set the precedent. He demonstrated His method of dealing with people without obscuring His message. He never asked His disciples to do something they had not seen Him do Himself.

The third general rule has to do with finding those who will then find others. Read these words from 2 Timothy 2:1–2: "You then, my son, be strong in the grace that is in Christ Jesus. And the things you have heard me say in the presence of many witnesses entrust to reliable men who will also be qualified to teach others." That is it. That is the point. Robert Coleman speaks of reproduction. Without connecting those we disciple with disciples of their own, our link with the future becomes again, a rope of sand. Jesus knowingly used images like the vine, branches, and fruit (John 15:1–11).

Jesus knew that He would never reach the masses Himself. The masses once persuaded for, could be twice persuaded against. Indeed, the great commission could read, "Go, preach, baptize, teach, but by all means—*make disciples.*" An excellent book by George Hunter entitled, *The Contagious Congregation,* makes this point powerfully and within the context of a fresh approach to church growth.

A WORD OF CAUTION

Discipleship means that in order for evangelism to work, it must be effective in the next generation. So, as a part of our follow-up, we seek to attach new Christains to the kind of body that will hold them accountable on a regular basis. This process is not without pitfalls, however.

We attach people to Jesus Christ, not to ourselves. In recent years, a type of discipleship program has emerged under the heading of "Shepherding." Many of the objectives within that program have been the same as we have already discussed. Trouble can arise with some such programs, however. On the whole I would encourage Christians to find someone to disciple them who lives close by and who can maintain contact, in person, on a regular basis. Itinerant (or traveling) shepherds might be well-meaning, but that kind of an arrangement too easily leads to the "guru-type" relationship. E. Stanley Jones adopted the Ashram (retreat) from the Hindu peoples, but he refused to be the guru, as was the Hindu custom. He insisted that Jesus Christ was the only guru for every Ashram.

The point here should be obvious. We must not attach ourselves to shepherds who would not point us to Jesus Christ. All shepherds, no matter how wise or discerning, are only sheep themselves. I have always been suspicious of shepherds who were not someone else's sheep. Who said it? "Shepherds do not beget sheep. Sheep beget sheep."

In a follow-up relationship, let the new Christian set the agenda. All too frequently the would-be discipler descends on the fledgling with almost omnipotent force. We do not realize what power we wield. New Christians, especially those we have had the privilege of leading to Christ, watch us closely. I have found that it is extremely important to avoid squeezing them into our own mold: "You must do this, or you must do that." Instead, I am finding that it is much more productive if we can trust those we seek to disciple to set their own agenda. Instead of "John, you have this problem," the solid relationship establishes enough trust for John to say, "Bob, I have this problem. Do you love me enough to pray for me daily and then hold me accountable with regard to its correction?"

True spirituality has to do with an awareness of God's presence in one's life. This is so important that much of the next chapter has been devoted to sorting it out. Since this is another problem area, a brief word needs to be stated, but this will also serve as an introduction to the chapter to follow.

For many years I believed that Christians followed a set of rules. If they obeyed this set of rules, they were Christians; if not, they were not. While this is true to a certain extent, one can never reduce Christianity to "do's and don't's." True spirituality is more than religious principle. It is more than a philosophy of life. It is a *way* of life, a dynamic relationship with a living God. True spirituality has to do with an awareness of God's presence in one's life. In follow-up, we need to encourage new Christians to speak with God and to read His Word, because He listens and His words are for us. True spirituality is not simply fulfilling some religious exercise, as if that is what Christianity is all about. Much more will be said about that shortly. For now, let us review what we have discussed thus far in Part IV.

Follow-up is vital to every Christian. We have a responsibility to those within our sphere of influence who might respond to us in a discipling relationship. Select a few. Model your teaching. Lead them to others so that the process continues. Attach them to the body of Christ, not to yourself. Let them set the agenda. Bring them to an awareness of God's presence in their lives. This is ministering. This is relational evangelism at its best.

Chapter 14
Follow-up Through Community

To evangelize is so to present Christ Jesus in the power of the Holy Spirit, that men shall come to put their trust in God through Him, to accept Him as their Saviour, and serve Him as their King in the fellowship of His church.

1918 Committee of Archbishops

Last week a student came into my office and asked the question: "What does it mean when Jesus says, 'Whatever you bind on earth will be bound in heaven, and whatever you loose on earth will be loosed in heaven.'" I replied with another question: "What is the context?" We turned to the passage together—Matthew 18:18. We found that that particular verse is a part of Jesus' advice concerning a brother who sins against you. As a last resort, make your appeal to the church. If your brother refuses to listen to the church, turn him out because whatever you (the church) bind or loose on earth will be bound or loosed in heaven. The larger context concerns Jesus' teaching on the kingdom of God. Within that kingdom stands the church militant and triumphant. To put this just a bit differently, whatever the church militant can bind to itself on earth becomes bound to the church triumphant in heaven.

The key is the church. To be a part of the kingdom is to be a part of the body—the church of Jesus Christ. We cannot afford to be cut off. In another place Jesus warns: "If anyone does not remain in me, he is like a branch that is thrown away and withers; such branches are picked up, thrown into the fire and burned" (John 15:6).

Discipleship, therefore, has a larger meaning. We not only disciple others, we make certain that they are properly attached to a vital community of believers who can assist them in their continuing victory over sin and death. Jesus gave the disciples one to another. The good news of the gospel is not only that God so loved us, but that we can love one another.

Let's look closer. Discipleship usually involves the one-on-one relationship. Beyond that the church, the community of believers, extends to the *ecclesiola* or "little churches" within the church and then to the larger body. All are vital to follow-up. They make the difference between binding and loosing, victory and defeat, life and death. We will look first to the little churches or small groups and then to the church as a larger or corporate body.

BUILDING COMMUNITY THROUGH SMALL GROUPS

Discipleship has more to do with direction and correction. Small groups have more to do with affirmation, acceptance, encouragement, and support. Both, however, involve discipline. John Wesley was fond of saying: "The body and soul make a man but the Spirit and discipline make a Christian." In fact, one of the most interesting passages in all of Wesley's writings describes the origin of the class meeting:

> It can scarce be conceived what advantages have been reaped from this little prudential regulation. Many now happily experienced that Christian fellowship of which they have not so much as an idea before. They began to "care for each other." As they had daily a more intimate acquaintance with, so they had a more endeared affection for, each other. And "speaking the truth in love, they grew up into him in all things, who is the Head, even Christ; from whom the whole body, fitly joined together, and compacted by that which every joint supplied, according to the effectual working in the measure of every part, increased unto the edifying itself in love.[1]

Wesley obviously draws heavily from the description of the church in Ephesians 4. He almost seems to be saying: This really works. If you will break down disciplined fellowship so that everyone present can experience it firsthand, a level of *koinonia* develops that otherwise is absent and unknown. Discipline surfaces within the closer fellowship unmatched even in a service of worship. John Wesley's groups or classes served several purposes. First of all they were extremely effective with regard to evangelism. Most of the people who were won to Christ during the eighteenth-century Evangelical Revival were actually won in these classes. This is also the place where baby Christians were both stabilized and then maintained. It was in these small groups that young converts were sensitized and then resensitized as to precisely what God was doing in their lives.

Recently I asked my son what God was doing in his life. Where was the cutting edge? What was God teaching him at the moment? He answered quickly: "Some of my friends want to know how close to the edge they can live without falling off. They want to know just how much sin they can commit and still be called Christian. God is teaching me that I do not need to live close to the edge, but close to the rock. I no longer ask whether or not something is sin. I ask whether or not something is the will of God. That way I do not have to worry so much about the edge." Quite frankly I was impressed with his response. It showed me that he was aware of what God was doing in his life. That is the function of the small group. Such groups have tremendous potential for developing our sensitivity both to sin and to holiness. Let me explain.

An awareness of sin. Sin is the great deceiver; it always promises that which it can never produce. Many an adventurer in the margin of society has been led astray by such deception. A vibrant fellowship sensitizes us to sin. Read carefully the following words from Hebrews 12:5–6: "And you have forgotten that word of encouragement that addresses you as sons: 'My son, do not make light of the Lord's discipline, and do not lose heart when he rebukes you, because the Lord disciplines those he loves, and he punishes everyone he accepts as a son.'"

How, then, does God discipline? The body of fellowship so sensitizes that God can discipline through the pangs of conscience. Perhaps your experience will bear this out as well. Suddenly I am aware of sin in my life and it grieves me. Listen, if you are suddenly aware of sin in your life, that is not simply cause for guilt and shame, but that is also cause for rejoicing because God is still treating you as a son or daughter. God's contempt of me would be that He was no longer offended by my sin. For me to be unaware of my sin would mean that God was no longer treating me as a son. So, we pray that God makes us keenly aware of that which separates, and then by the power of His Spirit, available through faith in Jesus Christ, He delivers us from bondage.

God's discipline is tough, but the world's discipline is far tougher. God's discipline saves us; the world's discipline buries us. I remember that before moving from the Los Angeles area a few years ago, I read an article in the *Los Angeles Times.* A young boy had been shot and killed by persons attempting to protect a "state's witness" who was being held for trial. The young boy was mistaken for an assassin. The words of the boy's mother have stayed with me: "I could never discipline him." God is not some kind of cosmic killjoy. The only reason He is against sin is that sin separates. Like the laws of nature, they can either work for us or against us. They can support a plane aloft, but if we jump out of that plane while in flight, we do not break the laws of gravity, they break us into tiny pieces. God cannot bear to see us destroy ourselves. He cannot bear to see His creation separated. It hurts us when members of our familys are separated. Why should God be any different? He is not only offended by our sin, He is grieved; so much so that He died in our place. So, "let us fix our eyes on Jesus, the author and perfecter of our faith, who for the joy set before him endured the cross, scorning its shame, and sat down at the right hand of the throne of God" (Heb. 12:2). Wesley insisted that we know no salvation without salvation from sin. We are not simply saved from hell, but from sin, because sin is the stuff that hell is made of. Lord, make us aware of sin. Discipline us. Treat us as sons and daughters, and enable us to respond to the power that delivers. That brings us to holiness.

An awareness of holiness. God's discipline not only makes us aware of sin, but of holiness as well. Again, Hebrews 12 says it: "For what son is not disciplined by his father? If you are not disciplined (and everyone undergoes discipline), then you are illegitimate children and not true sons. . . . Our fathers disciplined us for a little while as they thought best; but God disciplines us for our good, that we may share in his holiness. . . . Make every effort to live in peace with all men and to be holy; without holiness no one will see the Lord" (vv. 7, 8, 10, 14). New Christians need to realize that the righteousness imputed to them at conversion is then imparted to them through the *process* of sanctification. Wesley insisted that until imputed (the righteousness of Jesus Christ, attributed to us through faith in Him) becomes imparted (the righteousness of Jesus Christ, realized in us), we are not "ripe for glory." The former *entitles* us to heaven; the latter *qualifies* us for heaven. As new Christians are disciplined, they become more and more aware of sin and the resulting holiness binds them to God, themselves, and to those around them.

I just took a walk. As I was walking, I asked myself what holiness looks like. I remember a phrase out of my past: "How to reunite the two so long divided—knowledge and vital piety?" Vital piety—that is it! I remembered a few who impressed me with what I believed to be vital piety. It involved a quality of personhood. The piety *per se* never drew attention to itself. The persons I considered as having borne the marks of vital piety simply manifested a nature that I wanted to emulate. The piety that draws attention to itself too frequently stands out in the contrast to impiety. It smacks of hypocrisy. Genuine piety creates a quality of personhood that establishes itself in all walks of life. It is not so much dos and don't's, as a demeanor that makes it difficult to tell where the piety leaves off and the living begins. Small groups are the ideal place for modeling genuine, vital piety.

Within the fellowship of a small group, as friends share with us intimately and personally, we frequently become aware of God's intent for our lives. He creates in us a new being. We take on the mind of Christ, so that separation, at whatever level, is minimized. It feels good to feel good about God, ourselves, and those around us. It does not feel good not to feel good about God, ourselves, and those around us. Thus, as Christians, we are made aware of sin and holiness. This awareness is more than a state of acceptance; it is a quality of life that becomes more and more contagious. Holiness affects our character. Let me say just a bit more.

It seems as though I keep coming back to the character of the Christian in general and the evangelist in particular. If new Christians are to live victoriously so as to reproduce, they must be open to the God who dwells within them. I love these words from 1 Thessalonians 2:10–12, "You are witnesses, and so is God, of how holy, righteous, and blameless we were among you who believed. For you know that we dealt with each of you as a father deals with his own children, encouraging, comforting and urging you to live lives worthy of God, who calls you into his kingdom and glory."

Holiness is not simply an absence of sin, but the presence of good. God's sacrifice was far more than an innocent absence of evil, but an intentional presence of good, lived out in the God/man Jesus. If innocence was all that was required of the One who died for us, then Herod's sword might well have made the sacrifice in Bethlehem's manger, long before Calvary. No, holiness is an active participation with God, who dwells within us. Practicing His presence not only releases the resource but establishes the goal. That brings us to the larger or corporate body.

BUILDING COMMUNITY THROUGH THE LARGER BODY

This, too, seems to be a recurring theme. Sometimes persons ask me what I mean by the church. My answer is simple. The church is a body of believers gathered by the Holy Spirit into community. A church gathered is the church imbued with the Spirit's fruit, empowered by the Spirit's gifts, and launched by the Spirit's vision for kingdom living in a world alienated from God. The church *is* the body of Christ. She carries His cross. She reveals His love. She manifests His wisdom. She dies His death. She shares His resurrection. She witnesses His glorification. She predicts His return. She anticipates His kingdom come on earth as it is in heaven.

New Christians must be gathered. Earlier we spoke of discipling, where the new Christian is attached to someone else who would direct and correct within a loving relationship. More than that, the new Christian needs contact with the larger body. New Christians need exposure to the Word and sacraments as an experience of worship and praise. The small group makes us aware of sin and holinesss as we are sensitized and resensitized to what God is doing in our lives by the direct encounter with our closest friends. The larger body, however, has far greater resources for worship.

Worship as practicing the presence of God. In the seventeenth century a man named Nicolas Herman sought to punish himself for his own ineptness by exiling himself to a monastery. He was so clumsy that those in charge thought he would do the least harm in the kitchen. Nicolas loved God, and among mounds and mounds of potatoes he learned to keep a constant awareness of God's presence in his life. He later wrote a little book entitled *Practicing the Presence of God.* It became a classic under his new name—Brother Lawrence of the Resurrection.

Frank Laubach tells us that for two months he sought to keep his attention constantly on God. At the end of his experience he exclaimed: "Keeping my mind constantly upon

God was the most difficult thing of all. Everything else came easy!"

In my own experience it is most difficult for me to sin when I am most keenly aware of the presence of God. It is not easy to sin (although I sometimes manage) when I am aware that God is near. Sometimes it is almost as if I ask God to turn aside while I "indulge my carnal nature." I never feel comfortable doing that, however. Fortunately my conversion, if it did nothing else, spoiled my ability to rationalize sin. I know what sin is. I know that it separates me from God, from myself, and from those around me. Anything that does that is sin—no more, no less. The new Christian needs to be made aware of sin, and of holiness, but most of all of God.

Christianity (or more specificially true spirituality) was described in the last chapter negatively as *not* so many dos and don't's. Positively, true spirituality has almost everything to do with an awareness of God's presence in one's life. The depth of my devotion, the measure of my obedience, and the effectiveness of my witness are directly related to the intensity of my awareness of God's presence in my life. For that reason, I try never simply to preach sermons to be remembered. I try to preach sermons to create a moment, a moment when those within the corporate body are keenly aware of God in their midst. Now, that is worship! That is Christianity at its core. That is where it all begins; and that is where (if we fight the good fight, if we finish the race) it all ends.

Again, *community is vital for follow-up.* Baby Christians must be attached. True, they need to be discipled, but equally important they need a fellowship. At some point that fellowship must be small enough (a small group) so that we are aware of what God is doing in our lives (the awareness of sin and holiness). It must also be large enough so that we can experience worship. The larger body always has greater resources for knowing the mind of Christ. It is within that larger body that we become most keenly aware of the presence of God. God is in our midst. He is at work in our lives.

Get singled out; get picked off. This chapter has sought to make the transition from the one-on-one discipling relationship described previously to small groups, to the larger community (especially in worship) without diminishing the importance of *all three* for follow-up. No one can risk it alone. Thirteen entire chapters in the Book of Revelation relate to three and a half years of the Tribulation. Why? The apostle John wanted to impress on the churches of Asia the importance of unity. Persecution will come and devour the unattached. Get singled out; get picked off. John Wesley makes the same point when he describes mob violence against the revival efforts throughout his *Journal.* Why? Wesley wants to impress upon the people called Methodist the importance of unity. Persecution will come and devour the unattached. Get singled out; get picked off. We live in an age of similar but more subtle persecution. The message, therefore, is the same. Get singled out; get picked off. We are not just indispensable to the body, the body is indispensable to us as well.

---

[1]John Wesley, *Works,* 3rd ed. (Zondervan Reprint, n.d.), Vol. 8, p. 254.

Chapter 15
Follow-up, the Role of the Spirit

To evangelize is to present Christ Jesus to sinful men in order that through the power of the Holy Spirit, they may *come to put their trust in God through Him.* *J. I. Packer*

Ultimately, the Holy Spirit is the great evangel. In fact, the work of the Holy Spirit is so vital to the ministry of evangelism as a whole, that the present chapter will serve, in some sense, as a review for the entire book.

FROM BEGINNING TO END

On the eve of the crucifixion, Jesus said to His disciples: "When the Counselor comes, whom I will send to you from the Father, the Spirit of truth who goes out from the Father, he will testify about me; but you also must testify, for you have been with me from the beginning" (John 15:26, 27).

I prefer to speak about the work of the Holy Spirit in the life of the "believer" from beginning to end, from conception until death, in terms of *grace.* John Wesley spoke of prevenient grace, justifying grace, and sanctifying grace. Prevenient grace described the work of the Holy Spirit at work in the life of the "believer" between conception and conversion. Justifying grace described the work of the Holy Spirit in the life of the believer at the moment of conversion. Sanctifying grace described the work of the Spirit in the life of the believer between conversion and death.

Prevenient Grace

Most of us realize that prior to our conversions, the Holy Spirit is at work in our lives. Christians have long debated how this takes place. Roman Catholics refer to this work of the Spirit as "habitual grace," which is available to all within the *church,* and finds its focus in the sacraments. Protestants within the Reformed tradition refer to a "special grace," which is available only to the *elect,* and is irresistible. Their focus is on the Word and sacraments. Protestants within the Arminian tradition refer to this work of the Spirit prior to conversion as "prevenient grace," which is available to *everyone,* but is resistible. Their focus is on the Word, sacraments, and response. Prevenient grace for them is that work of the Holy Spirit supernaturally restoring all of us to a measure of free-will, wooing us, preventing us from moving so far from the way that when we finally understand the claims of the gospel on our lives, we are guaranteed the freedom to say yes. *It is God's initiative guaranteeing the freedom of our own response.* The point is that the Holy Spirit plays a major role in every tradition in bringing people to Christ. God pursues us by His Spirit. In an age when much of our teaching and preaching smacks once again of works righteousness, this is a vital corrective. Surely, "We love God because he *first* loved us." Let's look at a few biblical illustrations.

Earlier we alluded briefly to God already at work in the world before the evangelistic task is even begun. Let's look even closer to those same examples as they relate to the work of the Spirit. In Acts 8:29–40, for example, we find the story of the eunuch. The Spirit put Philip where He could use him (v. 29). The Spirit had already prepared the way (v. 30). He worked the change in baptism (v. 38). And he took Philip away (v. 39). In Acts 10:17–48 we find the story of Cornelius. The Spirit put Peter there (v. 19). He had already prepared the way (v. 24). He worked a change in baptism (vv. 44–48). He kept Peter there (v. 48). It is the Holy Spirit who works the change. This is especially evident in times of revival where He does not take sides, *He takes over.* So, our calling is to obedience. We harvest where He is already harvesting. What a joy to realize that although we can change nothing, He loves us enough to allow us to be midwife to change. A midwife, however, needs to know what she is doing. Do you remember the hysterical girl in *Gone With the Wind?* The new Christians need to be trained for this important ministry.

It is interesting to me that *paraclete* (translated "Comforter" or "Counselor" in most translations) is used in secular literature to refer to the one who stands next to another about to enter battle and says: "Sic 'em!" I am not sure, however, just how literally we should make that application, but the point for expanding our understanding of the role of the Holy Spirit in evangelism is already made.

The New Testament church was a band of new Christians "chattering" the gospel. They were Spirit-filled believers, a witnessing community. The Spirit of God increased their quality and their quantity daily.

Justifying Grace

I frequently preach on Ephesians 2:8: "For it is by grace you have been saved, through faith—and this not from yourselves, it is the gift of God." Thus far we have dealt briefly with the theology of prevenient grace. That is a necessary foundation. Prevenient grace guarantees the integrity of an evangelistic appeal. Since any appeal calls for response, it is obviously important to be able to make such a response. We must now turn to the larger picture, however, and to the appeal itself. By grace (prevenient grace) through faith constitutes the heart of the gospel message.

John Wesley tells us that he preached basically three kinds of sermons. To the unawakened (those not yet convicted of sin), he spoke mainly of death and hell. To those awakened (but not yet converted), he spoke mainly of faith. To those converted, he spoke mainly of perfection or entire sanctification. Let's, for a moment, focus at the point of his evangelistic appeal—to those awakened. Faith is the key. Wesley goes to great lengths to define it. He tells us what it is not. It is not that faith of a heathen, nor of a devil, nor even that of the apostles while Chrit remained in the flesh.[1] He tells us what it is. It is, in a general sense, "a divine supernatural, *evidence* or *conviction,* 'of things not seen,' not discoverable by our bodily senses, as being either past, future, or spiritual. Justifying faith implies, not only a divine evidence or conviction that 'God was in Christ, reconciling the world unto himself;' but a sure trust and confidence that Christ died for *my* sins, that He loved *me* and gave Himself for *me*."[2] Then the passage following this statement provides a further key. There he speaks of *repentence.*[3] Wesley's evangelistic thrust insisted that faith build upon a firm foundation. The repentance that lead to faith was for Wesley what I sometimes refer to as the "I give up." Let me explain using Wesley's own life as the illustration.

It is my conviction that Wesley's "instantaneous" conversion experience took thirteen years to manifest itself fully. The reason for the delay was that it took him considerable effort to divest himself of the bankruptcy of his own works-righteousness. Wesley, just prior to Aldersgate (his evangelical conversion), included in his journal these words from a letter written from John Gambold to his brother Charles prefacing them with the statement that he found them "so true." Gambold writes: "The doctrine of faith is a downright robber. It takes away all this wealth, and only tells us it is deposited for us with somebody else, upon whose bounty we must live like mere beggars. Indeed, they are truly beggars, vile and filthy sinners till very lately, many stoop to live in this dependent condition: It suits them well enough. But they who have long distinguished themselves from the herd of vicious wretches, or have even gone beyond *moral* men; for them to be told that they are either not so well, but the same needy, impotent, insignificant vessels of mercy with the others: This is more shocking to reason than transubstantiation."[4]

Even before leaving for Georgia as a missionary (two and a half years before Aldersgate), Wesley sensed that something was amiss. At that point he attempted to exchange the outward works of "visiting the sick or clothing the naked" for the inward works of a pursuit of holiness "or a union of a soul with God." He comments later that "in this refined way of trusting to my own works and my own righteousness (so zealously inculcated by the mystic writers), I dragged on heavily, finding no comfort or help therein."[5] At long last Wesley resolved to seek salvation through faith by first of all "absolutely renouncing all dependence, in whole or in part, upon *my own* works or righteousness; on which I had really grounded my hope of salvation, though I knew it not, from my youth up."[6] This was the point at which Wesley "gave up." His besetting sin was a misplaced trust. He repented. He gave up his faith in his own self-righteousness and determined to trust Christ alone as his "sole justification, sanctification, and redemption." Aldersgate followed shortly thereafter.

For the rest of his life this "I give up," this (to use the words of á Kempis) "following naked the naked Jesus" became the spearhead for his evangelistic appeal. His watchwords included such warnings as: "Do not trust that broken reed of your infant baptism. Do not trust anyone or anything else for salvation apart from Christ." He writes: "As 'there is no other name given under heaven,' than that of Jesus of Nazareth, no other merit whereby a condemned sinner can ever be saved from the guilt of sin; so there is no other way of obtaining a share of His merit, *than by faith in His name*."[7] This should provide a key for our own understanding of evangelism as well. Again, give it up! Trust Christ alone! He wants to bless us. Let me illustrate.

I have always thought it interesting that the word *pneuma* (Spirit) is the translation of *ruach* (wind) in the Greek translation of the Hebrew Old Testament. Wind equals Spirit and Spirit equals wind. That is no accidental metaphor. Most of us know that wind blows from high pressure to low pressure, to the point of least resistance. Likewise, the Holy Spirit (in this case prevenient and justifying grace) moves from high pressure to low pressure, to the point of least resistance, to the "I give up."

This is the key to the larger picture. Prevenient grace prepares us for repentance and belief. Our yes then creates low pressure so that the Holy Spirit no longer woos but rushes to the very center of our being creating and recreating after the mind of Christ. At this point allow an old evangelist a word of exhortation. You can take it. People the world over are being drawn by the Spirit of God. The prevenient grace of God is at work all around us. People, like Wesley, are weary of the bankruptcy of their own self-sufficiency. People are restless and uneasy. They cannot change their own lives. They cannot turn around. Most do not like doing what they do. Many are discontent with a form of godliness that denies the power to pull it off. They are weary of the law without strength or inclination to obey it. Encourage them to give up their vain attempts to save themselves. Ask them to place their faith and trust in Christ alone for salvation.

Sanctifying Grace

Beyond conversion the Holy Spirit operates to strengthen and sustain. Again, sanctifying grace refers to the work of the Spirit in the life of the believer between conversion and death. In a sense, *the Spirit Himself seeks to establish His own follow-up*. He not only saves us from hell, but from sin. He constantly seeks to plumb some new depth of our experience, to reveal some area of resistance. As we yield to Him,

He teaches us new things daily. For example, He gives us knowledge about God, about ourselves, and about those around us. Let me illustrate.

The knowledge of God is not easy to write about. Allow me to make a few general observations in order to underscore the role of the Spirit in follow-up. During the last century many theologians believed that all knowledge of God had to submit to their own ability to reason. You started with your experience (cause) and then worked up to an understanding of God (effect).

During this century many theologians have taken exception to that view. Perhaps the most prominent is Karl Barth. Barth insists that all knowledge of God must ultimately be revealed. Our natural ability to reason is inadequate for any knowledge beyond our own senses. Thus, the Holy Spirit is the only One who can teach us about God. These words say it well: "The Spirit searches all things, even the deep things of God. For who among men knows the thoughts of a man except the man's spirit within him? In the same way no one knows the thoughts of God except the Spirit of God. We have not received the spirit of the world, but the Spirit who is from God, that we may understand what God has freely given us. This is what we speak, not in words taught us by human wisdom, but in words taught by the Spirit, expressing spiritual truths in spiritual words" (1 Cor. 2:10–13).

Knowledge of ourselves can also be an issue of spiritual discernment. Although we are not limited to the Spirit (as with the knowledge of God), the Spirit best reveals who we are. Recently a friend of mine and I sat alone in a park. He gave me an interesting description of himself as revealed by the Spirit. He had had some disagreement with a friend, and he had prayed that God would plead his case in the mind of his friend, since he had not been able to penetrate the separation. Then (as God would have it), the Spirit revealed to my friend the case of his adversary. He realized his own failure and an interesting emotion took over. Rather than wallow in guilt and shame, my friend felt refreshed. Suddenly he felt that something could be done. Frustration often arises when hopelessness sets in. We feel helpless. Now he felt different. He saw his friend differently. He experienced joy, knowing that reconciliation was now a possibility. The result? He went to his friend; he shared his own failure. He asked his friend for forgiveness and was dumbfounded, for the Spirit had worked where he could not work and healing took place in a moment.

Knowing others can also be the work of the Spirit. Everyone has a story to tell. As Christians, we can mean well, but lack the understanding to minister effectively. Recently a student lost a baby through crib death. One well-meaning comforter said: "I know how you feel. I have a baby at home." The couple's reaction? "No, you don't; your baby is alive, while ours is dead." The truth is, we do not know how that student and his wife felt—even if we have lost babies of our own. We may remember how we felt, but we do not really know how they feel because we do not know who they are. We do not know how they handle grief. We do not know how they view death. I remember talking to the couple myself. The mother made what I felt was a profound statement. Most of their comfort came from the psalms. Before their tragic experience, she had not understood why some of the words of the psalms were included in a certain order. After their experience, it all began to make sense. The Spirit of God had taken those words, written so many years ago, and applied them to their situation, almost as if the Spirit had had them in mind when they were written. Is that hard to believe? I think not. Similarly, the Spirit gives us understanding far beyond our own wisdom and speaks to the needs of others, that we might be the body of Christ—a community, "the company of the committed."

SERVING OTHERS

Sometimes we do not realize that the Spirit of God will follow up His own work by then providing the new convert with an opportunity for ministry. I used to think it was a simple task to prepare Christian ministers. All we had to do was to find motivated Christians and train them to minister. Do you know what I found? Some ministerial students in the midst of their training, lost their Christianity. At first I felt responsible. Perhaps my classes were raising more questions than they were answering. I have always felt that it was important to put more in the bucket than goes out. I had to raise questions. I had to force students to think theologically. I had to challenge them. As I pressed some students to tell me why they had felt their faith diminish while in seminary, two areas were quickly conspicuous. The first was fellowship. The second was service. Let me say more.

Seminary students, like many young Christians, feel that the sole key to continuing a vital relationship with God involves prayer and Bible reading. While this is crucial, it was not their reason for losing faith. Most had continued in some form of private devotion. The most obvious reason for the dimunition of their first love had to do with a loss of fellowship within a caring community. They had left their home churches and had failed to establish weekly ties in their new setting. In light of what has been said already, the reasons for fellowship should now be fairly apparent. The Spirit of God has chosen to work primarily through a body. He attaches us to a "momma." A second reason for a loss of faith that might not be so apparent, however, has to do with service.

Many of us do not realize how important it is to serve others. The Holy Spirit equips us to minister. If we do not give it away, we get spiritually puffy. Little wonder Jesus says: "Whoever wants to become great among you must be your servant, and whoever wants to be first must be slave of all. For even the Son of Man did not come to be served, but to serve, and to give his life as a ransom for many" (Mark 10:43–45).

Many students come to seminary to prepare for ministry, and during their time of study lose contact with the kind of service that motivated them to begin with. Faith shrivels when it is not given away. One of the greatest principles of Christianity is that in order to receive, we must give, give, give. Jesus speaks of lighted candles and the salt of the earth. The message is always the same. The Holy Spirit draws us into fellowship one with another, and then equips us to serve others by the power at work within us. That power will frequently manifest itself through gifts.

Every Christian has gifts. These gifts normally surface within the context of ministry. To put it another way, our natural sphere of influence usually determines our supernatural gifts. In other words, our supernatural gifts equip us to minister effectively within our natural sphere of influence. God is forever equipping and enabling the Christian in ministry. So, how do we know what our gifts are? We start doing ministry and then see what gifts begin to surface.

The gifts of the Holy Spirit rarely surface outside the context of ministry. If I dare to step out in faith in ministry, the gifts necessary to fulfill that ministry will manifest themselves. As Christians we must trust God for that. He will not disappoint us. Admittedly some types of ministry seem too big for us—terrific! God will supply our needs. I am asking you to believe it and to act on it. Faith has been compared to the filament in a light bulb. Even when the filament broken, the power is still there but it simply refuses to shine. The same thing could be said for evangelism. The power to effect change in the hearts and lives of others is there. The filament is complete when we act upon our calling and the light goes on.

Again, *our natural sphere normally determines our supernatural gifts.* There are, however, some exceptions to that. Occasionally our supernatural gifts determine our natural sphere of influence. There are some spheres where there is no one to minister naturally. In these instances God will raise someone up and bestow gifts on them with a particular sphere in mind. God called Moses and gave him gifts necessary to speak to the Egyptians. God called Paul and gave him gifts necessary to speak to the Gentiles. God called David Wilkerson and gave him gifts necessary to speak to the toughs in Harlem. And on its goes.

In conclusion, let's say it again. The Holy Spirit woos, converts, sanctifies, gathers, and disperses for service to the world, that the world might know one again its created image—the image of God—Father, Son, and Holy Spirit. Evangelism is Pentecost refusing to let the sun set on Easter Sunday. Hallelujah and Amen!

---

[1]John Wesley, *Works,* 3rd ed. (Zondervan Reprint, n.d.), Vol 5, pp. 8f.
[2]*Words,* 3rd ed. Vol. 5, pp. 60f.
[3]*Words,* 3rd ed. Vol. 5, p. 61.
[4]*Words,* 3rd ed. Vol. 1, p. 96.
[5]*Words,* 3rd ed. Vol. 1, p. 100.
[6]*Words,* 3rd ed. Vol. 1, p. 102.
[7]*Words,* 3rd ed. Vol. 5, p. 61.

Chapter 16
A Case Study

This case attempts to demonstrate the importance of a relationship for follow-up.

FOR OLD TIME'S SAKE

Jerry Adams sat waiting for the phone to ring. It had been nearly two years since he had seen Jake, an old friend out of a disappointing past. It was Sunday night, a time usually reserved for church, but Jerry had placed a fleece. If Jake called before 7:00 P.M. (as he had promised to do) he would spend the evening with him, visiting some of their old haunts—just for old time's sake.

Background

Even as a non-Christian, Jerry's rebellion quotient (what he referred to his "RQ") had never been very high. His greatest sin had always been somewhat of a bore to most of his friends. He had, on occasion, had a beer, and had smoked dope a time or two, but nothing much more serious than that. Yet, until two years ago, he had been restless and uneasy. Something had been missing. He had been in his senior year in college and was confronted with the decision of what to do with the rest of his life. Jake and the rest of his fraternity brothers seemed content to climb ladders and chase dollars. Jerry felt that life had to have more of a challenge than that. He wanted his future to count for something. Then, in October of his senior year he had become close friends with Eric.

Eric Jasson was another name out of Jerry's past. They had gone to high school together, but had run in different circles. They had always liked each other, but a relationship had never developed. During their early college years, they were aware of each other, but again there was no real friendship. Then, in the midst of Jerry's vocational struggle, he and Eric had bumped into each other in the "Cellar," a snackshop in the basement of the Student Union. Jerry never forgot that initial conversation.

Jerry had actually taken the lead. Eric had been sitting alone at the table writing. Jerry approached him with the usual remarks: "Eric, how have you been? This place is so big, I hardly ever see you except across the quad." Eric replied, with remarkable enthusiasm: "Jerry, I'm okay, thanks for asking. Sit down and join me if you have a moment. Tell me about yourself." Jerry sat down and he unloaded. For some reason, he found himself sharing all the frustration, the fear, and the anxiety about his future plans. Although the resumés had been mailed and the contacts been made, the job market was tight. In a few short months he would be on his own. The competition for top jobs was fierce. Eric listened carefully. Then he responded. At first, he spoke hesitantly. Then the words seemed to flow straight from Eric to Jerry. The gist of those words was this. All of the ingredients causing the frustration and fear in Jerry's mind were in Eric's also, but with one major difference. Eric did not seem frustrated. He seemed excited about his future. Again, the resumés had gone out and the contacts had been made, so there was nothing left to do, which causes many people to experience frustration. They feel helpless and tossed by some mindless wind of fate. Yet, Eric expressed a sense of joy and accomplishment. He appeared at ease, even expectant. Jerry did not probe, but remained interested. Eric then shared the reason for his optimism.

In a low key but convincing manner, Eric told Jerry about his call to ministry. Oh, it was not ministry in the ordained sense, but it was ministry none the less. He had committed his life to God. Some years earlier he had placed his faith and trust in Jesus Christ. Although he had studied hard and had made all of the contacts humanly possible, good or bad, his future was now God's problem. Eric believed that God cared and wanted to place him in the spot where he could best serve people. His gifts were not extraordinary, by any means, but he felt that someone "out there" needed him. Moments, no hours later, Jerry found himself opening up even more.

Over the next few months the two young men became fast friends. Jerry was always amazed at how Eric would express appreciation for Jerry's gifts and do so convincingly. He was also impressed with his apparent unshakable faith in the face of disappointment after disappointment as job opportunities fell through one after another. Then it happened. Jerry had just been offered the job of his dreams. Yet, he was still uneasy. Eric's peace and joy were still evident. Eric seemed more pleased with the prospect of Jerry's job than Jerry did. Then, late one night, Jerry responded to Eric's challenge to put his faith and trust in Jesus Christ. Boom! The house was no longer empty. Jerry, for the first time in his life, felt motivated, really motivated. He wanted his job to count for God. He found himself sharing in Eric's excitment about the future, and not just for his own, but for Eric's as well. Ironically it was one of Jerry's leads that landed Eric a job in the same company where Jerry was to work.

Where the Rubber Hits the Road

Jerry and Eric had maintained a discipling relationship for two years. Eric had married, but Jerry was included in many of the family activities. Jerry had matured rapidly in his faith. God had consecrated his job, so that he was able to see ministry at work from 9 to 5. He had led several of his colleagues to Christ. He had even helped Eric and his new bride work through some problem areas in their marriage.

Jerry, Eric, and a couple of others were in a discipling relationship, and had joined a church. Jerry had advanced even faster in his career than Eric. All seemed to be going so well. Then a couple of setbacks occurred. First, Jerry had fallen in love, but it had not worked out. After a two-month engagement, the relationship had broken up, and Jerry felt abandoned by God. Suddenly (and for no apparent reason) he felt weary of Eric. He began to skip some of their weekly gatherings. About this same time a division had rocked the church. Their pastor had left for another pastorate, and a power struggle had ensued over the selection of his successor. Jerry had become less involved in church as well.

Jake Martin

The previous day Jerry had landed a new account for the company. Jake Martin, a fraternity brother from college, had signed a lucrative contract. Jake was in town for a few days and had promised to phone Jerry the next evening so that they could "make the rounds"—for old time's sake. Jerry was surprised to feel the old juice begin to rise. That morning he had gone to church and had shared with Eric what a great opportunity this would be to witness to Jake. Yet, down deep, Jerry knew that this was a crossroad. He was on the brink of surging ahead or falling back into an old lifestyle. Try as he could to rationalize the prospect, he knew that he might well be in trouble in his present state of mind. Eric's only response had been that he should enter those relationships where he could give more than they would take. If Jerry's influence *for* the life of Christ would not outweigh Jake's influence *against,* he should probably back off until he was stronger. It was, of course, Jerry's decision. Then, that afternoon, Eric had phoned Jerry to say that he loved him, no matter what happened. Jerry could not mess up bad enough to make him love him any less.

As Jerry sat by the phone, his fleece was suddenly no longer the issue. What should he do? How could he know if the relationship would take more from him than he could give to it? Why didn't Eric tell him plainly what to do?

At 6:15, the phone rang. "Hello, Jerry, this is your old buddy, Jake. . . ."

DISCUSSION GUIDE

This case demonstrates both the ups and downs of relational evangelism. Let's assume that Jerry was soundly converted. Eric had followed up as best he could. Yet, as is often the case, disappointment frequently leads to temptation. It happens to all of us.

Questions

1. What about Eric's advice?
2. Is Jerry ready for Jake?
3. If so, what is the appropriate response?
4. If not, what is the appropriate response?
5. How should Eric follow up now?

CONCLUSION

This book has been an attempt to understand evangelism as a process of relationships. Genuine relationships are never for a moment. They continue across the months and sometimes years. Evangelism is more than "leading someone to Christ"—it is faithfully proclaiming the gospel at many different points in an individual's life. Let me illustrate.

I received a phone call from a friend who is now a minister of the gospel. In a book written over more than ten years ago, I told the story of this friend. At that time he had just given his life to Jesus Christ after twenty-eight years in prison. I remember visiting him the day after his conversion. He met me at the bars of his cell. The first works out of his mouth were : "Tuttle, I laid awake last night thinking. Suddenly it occurred to me that it takes an average of twenty-five different witnesses before any real encounter with God takes place, and just because you were number 25, you think you did it all when 24 just as important, went before you." I confess, he got me. That can be a problem with us evangelicals. If we see the change take place, we think that we did it all when 24, just as important, went before us. The opposite to this is also a problem. Many of us refuse to be affirmed in ministry if we do not see the change take place before our eyes. We deliver a faithful witness only to go home thinking: "She did not receive Christ. I really blew it." My prayer for you is that you will receive just as much affirmation in being 1 to 24 (or 26 to 50 for that matter) as in being number 25. Evangelism involves a host of decisions throughout one's life., Ultimately evangelism culminates not in conversion, but in death when we see the glory of God face to face.

Recently a young man came to my office confessing his loss of faith in God. The fire had gone out. He had suffered disappointment after disappointment in life. He had worked himself to the point of nervous exhaustion. He was spent. As he sat across from me I asked him several questions. I began: "What do you think of Jesus? Did He exist?" He replied that he did not know. I asked: "Do you believe that Julius Caesar existed?" He answered: "Of course." I reminded him that there was more hard evidence for the existence of Jesus than for Caesar. He replied: "Oh, I believe there was such a man." I asked: "Tell me about Him." He thought for a moment: "Well, He was a good man who wanted to help people." I asked: "Was He a liar?" The immediate reply: "No." I continued: "Why did they crucify Him?" Again he replied: "He claimed to be God's Son." I said: "If He was not a liar then it appears to me that He was who He said He was or He was mad. Was He mad?" The reply: "No, He certainly did not act like a madman. Too much of what He said and did have the ring of truth." I concluded: "If He lived, if He was not a liar, if He was not mad, why not believe He was who He said He was? Your faith in God is so closely attached to your present state of mind that you are having difficulty separating the two. You may need to go back to the basics. Extreme emotional instability sometimes affects our ability to believe beyond sight." I invited him to place his full attention once again on Jesus. To renew our trust in Him as Lord is to find new perspective for life as a whole. I must confess that I was not too surprised to see the young man respond. I sensed God's presence in our midst. The young man began to see hope. His faith was renewed.

Fortunately, that is not the end of the story. We began to talk about planting his small seed in good earth. He was no longer associating with Christian friends and was attending no church. I volunteered to see him in a discipling relationship and invited him to attend church with me on Sunday. There he would be cared for lovingly.

This is a true story. I tell it to you as it happened. As I thought about it, I realized that here is the book in review. The core, "Jesus is Lord," renewed this young man's vision for life. He was in my sphere of influence. I understood his struggle. His need surfaced in a relationship. Follow-up was assured because I see him almost daily and we will meet weekly. He will be asked to join a small group in our church. I believe that he will survive.

Let me close with a brief word of exhortation. I ask you to consider developing guidelines for understanding the core of the gospel. Will you become sensitive to your sphere of influence? Will you risk relationships out of which ministry can happen? Will you practice follow-up? Will you trust God to fill you with His Holy Spirit? If you will, I believe that you will become a more effective evangelist for Jesus Christ. You are precious and important. You are indispensable to the body of Christ. Believe it, receive it, act upon it, but most of all realize again and again, that someone out there needs you.

BIBLIOGRAPHY

THE CONTEMPORARY CONTEXT FOR EVANGELISM

Anderson, J. N. D. *Christianity and Comparative Religion*. Downers Grove, IL: Inter-Varsity, 1970.

Engels, James and Norton, Wilbert. *"What's Gone Wrong With the Harvest,"* Grand Rapids: Zondervan, 1975.

Guinness, Os. *The Dust of Death*. Downers Grove, IL: Inter-Varsity, 1973.

Johnston, Arthur. *The Battle for World Evangelism*. Wheaton: Tyndale, 1978

Schaeffer, Francis. *The Church at the End of the 20th Century*. Downers Grove, IL: Inter-Varsity, 1970.

Smith, Robert W., ed. *Christ and the Modern Mind*. Downers Grove, IL: Inter-Varsity, 1972.

IN DEFENSE OF THE FAITH

Anderson, J. N. D. *Christianity: The Witness of History*. London: Tyndale, 1969.

______. *The Evidence for the Resurrection*. Downers Grove, IL: Inter-Varsity, 1966.

Bruce, F. F. *Are the New Testament Documents Reliable?* Downers Grove, IL: Inter-Varsity.

Johnson, Robert. *The Meaning of Christ*. Philadelphia: Westminster, 1958.

Lewis, C. S. *Mere Christianity*. New York: Macmillan, 1952. (Also paperback.)

McDowell, Josh. *Evidence That Demands a Verdict*. San Bernadino, CA: 1972. Campus Crusade for Christ, 1972.

______ . *More Evidence That Demands a Verdict*, San Bernadino, CA: Campus Crusade for Christ, 1975.

Ramm, Bernard, L. *The God Who Makes a Difference*. Waco, TX: Word, 1972.
Schaeffer, Francis. *The God Who Is There*. Downers Grove, IL: Inter-Varsity, 1968.

THE BIBLICAL AND THEOLOGICAL BASIS OF EVANGELISM

Barth, Marcus, *The Broken Wall*. Valley Forge, PA: Judson, 1959.
Ford, Leighton. *One Way to Change the World*. New York: Harper and Row, 1970.
Green, Michael. *Evangelism in the Early Church*. Grand Rapids: Eerdmans, 1970.
Kraemer, Hendrick. *A Theology of the Laity*. Philadelphia: Westminster, 1958.
Kuiper, R. B. *God-Centered Evangelism*. Grand Rapids: Baker, 1961.
Packer, J. I. *Evangelism and the Sovereignty of God*. Downers Grove, IL: Inter-Varsity, 1961
______. *Knowing God*. Downers Grove, Il.: Inter-Varsity, 1973.
Peters, George. *A Biblical Theology of Missions*. Chicago: Moody, 1972.
Watson, David. *I Believe in Evangelism*. Grand Rapids: Eerdmans, 1977.

THE GOOD NEWS WE SHARE IN EVANGELISM

International Congress on World Evangelization. *Let the Earth Hear His Voice*, 1974.
Miller, Keith. *The Becomers*. Waco, TX: Word, 1973.
______. *The Taste of New Wine*. Waco, TX: Word, 1965.
Spurgeon, Charles. *The Soul Winner*. (with Foreword by Helmut Thielicke), Grand Rapids; Eerdmans, 1963.
Stedman, Ray. *Authentic Christianity*. Waco, TX: Word, 1975.
Stott, John R. W. *Basic Christianity*. Grand Rapids: Eerdmans, 1958.

EVANGELISM THROUGH PERSONAL WITNESS

Adams, Lane. *First Steps: A Follow-up Program for New Christians*. Waco, TX: Creative Resources.
______. *Come, Fly With Me*. Waco, TX: Word, 1975.
Anderson, Ken. *A Coward's Guide to Witnessing*. Carol Stream, IL: Creation House, 1972.
Augsburger, David. *Communicating Good News*. Newton, KS: Faith and Life Press, 1972.
Chafin, Kenneth L. *The Reluctant Witness*. Nashville: Broadman Press, 1974.
Coleman, Robert. *They Meet the Master*. Huntingdon Valley: Christian Outreach, 1973.

Eims, Leroy. *Winning Ways*. Wheaton: Victor, 1974.
Green, Bryan. *The Practice of Evangelism*. New York: Scribner, 1951.
Kennedy, James. *Evangelism Explosion*. Wheaton: Tyndale, 1970.
Little, Paul. *How to Give Away Your Faith*. Downers Grove, IL: Inter-Varsity, 1966.
Little, Paul E. *Know Why You Believe*. Downers Grove, IL: 1968. Leader's Guide available.
Martin, Robert J. *All About Witnessing*. Grand Rapids: Baker, 1975.
Rinker, Rosalind. *You Can Witness With Confidence*. Grand Rapids: Zondervan, 1962.

EVANGELISM THROUGH RELATIONSHIPS

Henricks, Howard. *Say It With Love*. Wheaton: Victor, 1972.
Hunt, Gladys. *It's Alive*. (Home Centered Bible Study Outreach) Wheaton: Harold Shaw, 1971.
Jauncey, James H. *Psychology for Successful Evangelism*. Chicago: Moody, 1973.
Larson, Bruce. *Setting Men Free*. Grand Rapids: Zondervan, 1967.
McPhee, Arthur G. *Friendship Evangelism*. Grand Rapids: Zondervan, 1979.
Miller, Keith, and Larson, Bruce. *The Edge of Adventure: An Experiment on Faith*. Waco, TX: Word, 1974.
Milliken, Bill. *Tough Love*. Old Tappan, NJ: Fleming H. Revell, 1968.
Raines, Robert A. *New Life in the Church*. New York: Harper and Row, 1961.
Shoemaker, Sam. *How You Can Help Other People*. Lay Renewal Publications, 1973.

ADVOCACY AND EVANGELISM

Fackre, Gabriel. *Do and Tell: Engagement Evangelism in the '70's*. Grand Rapids: Eerdmans, 1974.
Ford, Leighton, *The Christian Persuader*. New York: Harper and Row, 1966.
Milliken, Bill. *So Long, Sweet Jesus*. New York: Hawthorn (Dutton), 1973.
Moberg, David. *The Great Reversal*. Philadelphia: Lippincott, 1972.
______ . *Inasmuch*. Grand Rapids: Eerdmans, 1965.
Mott, John R. *The Larger Evangelism*, Nashville: Abingdon, n. d.
Mouw, Richard. *Political Evangelism*. Grand Rapids: Eerdmans, 1973.
O'Connor, Elizabeth. *Journey Inward, Journey Outward*. New York: Harper and Row, 1968.
Yoder, John Howard. *The Politics of Jesus*. Grand Rapids: Eerdmans, 1972.

EVANGELISM AND CHRISTIAN COMMUNITY

Bonhoeffer, Dietrich. *Life Together.* New York: Harper and Row, 1954.

Cosby, Gordon. *Handbook for Mission Groups.* Waco, TX: Word, 1975.

Howard, Walden. *Groups That Work.* Grand Rapids: Zondervan, 1968.

Johnson, David W. & Johnson, Frank P. *Joining Together: Group Theory and Group Skills.* Englewood Cliffs, NJ: Prentice Hall, 1975.

Miller, Paul. *Group Dynamics in Evangelism.* Scottsdale, PA: Herald, 1958.

Olsen, Charles. *The Base Church.* Atlanta: John Knox, 1973.

Richards, Lawrence O. *69 Ways to Start a Study Group and Keep it Growing.* Grand Rapids: Zondervan, 1973.

Stedman, Ray. *Body Life.* Glendale, CA: Regal, 1972.

EVANGELISM THROUGH THE LOCAL CONGREGATION

Edge, Findley B. *The Greening of the Church.* Waco, TX: Word, 1971.

Girard, Robert. *Brethren Hang Loose.* Grand Rapids: Zondervan, 1972.

Larson, Bruce and Ralph Osborne. *The Emerging Church.* Waco, TX: Word, 1970.

Mains, David. *Full Circle,* Waco, TX: Word, 1972.

Short, Roy L. *Evangelism Through the Local Church.* Nashville: Abingdon, 1956.

Sweazey, George E. *Effective Evangelism.* New York: Harper, 1953.

———. *The Church as Evangelist.* New York: Harper and Row, 1978.

Synder, Howard A. *The Problem of Wineskins.* Downers Grove, IL: Inter-Varsity, 1975.

EVANGELISM AND DISCIPLESHIP

Ayres, Francis. *The Ministry of the Laity.* Philadelphia: Westminster Press, 1962.

Coleman, Robert, *The Master Plan of Evangelism.* Huntingdon Valley: Christian Outreach, 1963.

Eims, Leroy. *Be the Leader You Were Meant to Be.* Wheaton: Victor, 1975.

Gibbs, Mark and T. Ralph Morton. *God's Frozen People.* Philadelphia: Westminster, 1965.

Henrichsen, Walter A. *Disciples Are Made Not Born.* Wheaton, Victor, 1974

Hunter, George, ed. *Rethinking Evangelism,* Tidings, 1971.

Hyde, Douglas. *Dedication and Leadership*. Notre Dame, IL: Notre Dame Press, 1966.

Kuhne, Gary W. *The Dynamics of Personal Follow-up*. Grand Rapids: Zondervan, 1976.

Miller, Chuck. *Now That I'm a Christian*. Glendale, CA: Regal, 1975.

Trueblood, Elton. *The Company of the Committed*. New York: Harper and Row, 1961.

Tuttle, Robert G., Sr. *Born Again: What Then?* Lima, OH: C. S. S. Publishing Co., 1980.

EVANGELISM AND PRINCIPLES OF CHURCH GROWTH

Donald Bridge and David Phypers. *Spiritual Gifts and the Church*. Downers Grove, IL: Inter-Varsity, 1973.

Hodges, Melvin L. *A Guide to Church Planting*. Chicago: Moody, 1973.

Hunter, George. *The Contagious Congregation*. Nashville: Abingdon, 1979.

McGavran, Donald. *Understanding Church Growth*. Grand Rapids: Eerdmans, 1970.

McGavran, Donald and Win Arn. *How To Grow A Church*. Glendale CA: Regal, 1973.

EVANGELISM AND THE HOLY SPIRIT

Edman, V. Raymond. *They Found the Secret*. Grand Rapids: Zondervan, 1960.

Tuttle, Robert G., Jr. *The Partakers*. Nashville: Abingdon, 1974.